THE GOSPEL OF
ST. JOHN

THE GOSPEL OF
ST. JOHN

By
RUDOLF STEINER

THE ANTHROPOSOPHIC PRESS, INC.
SPRING VALLEY   NEW YORK

A cycle of twelve lectures given at
Hamburg, May 18–31, 1908. Translated from shorthand reports unre-
vised by the lecturer, from the German
edition published with the title, *Das
Johannes-Evangelium* (Vol. 103 in the
Bibliographic Survey, 1961). Translated by Maud B. Monges.

This translation has been authorized
for the Western Hemisphere by the
Rudolf Steiner Nachlassverwaltung,
Dornach, Switzerland

Printed in the United States of America

TABLE OF CONTENTS

AN INTRODUCTION TO THE REFLECTIONS OF
RUDOLF STEINER ON THE GOSPEL OF ST. JOHN

By Marie Steiner

With this book we penetrate into the innermost structure of Rudolf Steiner's activities. For all of his endeavour had this one goal:—to pave for the world the way to the Christ. The Christ was lost for us during the period of rationalism and materialism. The churches yawned in desolate emptiness, and if one did not sit within them as an unmoved, childlike human being there was vacuity or contradiction in head and heart. What came from the lips of the exponent of Christian teaching did not bear the stamp of truth and conviction. Its effect was often hollow, puffed up, or sometimes mechanistic, at best stultifying. The church became conventional, a matter of form, accepting a compromise with science without being able to offset it with something truly effective. Gradually it was forced to withdraw its requirements of faith, because it could not present to the doubter enough that was factual to be able to change belief into sure conviction and knowledge. Candidates for confirmation had already been forced to withdraw their questions before the uncertainty and obvious side-stepping of the truth on the part of the revered pastor. Children who had left school found themselves standing before a spiritual void and felt the foundations of their souls give way beneath them. The Roman Catholic church frightened the Protestants away by its enslavement of freedom, and by the hollow mutterings of the celebrants of the churchly rites whose whole behaviour was often a mockery of what they were intended to represent. And yet, the forms gave evidence of something that had been lost. But where was it to be sought? Certainly not in the direction of modern science, for this had decreed limits to knowledge and functioned like the skull of a skeleton, hollow-eyed, severed from the trunk. Coherent life, the formative lines and the accomplishment were lacking. One could indeed become enthusiastic over the artistry of the individual parts, but the whole lacked hands and feet. It was only a fragment. The great cosmic tortoise of the Brahmanical religion, bearer of the earthly disc, produced in its imaginative force more pleasing effects. Men felt themselves surrounded by the rushing sound of the surging universal ether; they knew that there was something quite different from what is expressed in that cosmic image, something more than an automatically active mechanism, which out of itself sets the earth-wheel in motion—to which, by degrees, a meaning is given by equally automatically-created human beings—only to fall again into insensibility.

Something substantial was wafted over the world out of these ancient religions. If their path is followed, an ascent can be observed from a stifled and benumbed consciousness to ever lighter spheres of thought. Great cultures arose out of these religions; mighty imaginations passed from them over into the present time. Art and science developed within them, leaving sublime monuments behind. Here was a thread to follow which was a spiritual necessity. This thread was lost again and again in a mysterious obscurity. It led down through the temple places before which stood warning guardians who propounded questions and those who failed to answer suffered death. These were enigmatical words which finally culminated with the warning: "Know thou thyself!" This path had again to be discovered and illumined. But how to find it?

From the silent temples, whose doors were closed, traces of these teachings had escaped into the outer world. Their meaning became manifest in ever more powerfully developing civilizations which comprised increasingly larger and larger groups of human beings until at last the individual man emerged as a personality. No longer on the one side the God-inspired leader and teacher or sovereign, and on the other the dull people—but the separate human being, the personality who through his especial qualifications had become an individual. This occurred most gloriously in Greece where God and man approached one another. The supersensible was blended with the sensible in art. The individual personality had become mature. The Mysteries, however, withdrew, veiled themselves more deeply and their meaning, which formerly was wrapped in secrecy, and therefore secure and untouched by doubt, became hidden.

Human thought began to take its own course. Schools of Philosophy arose. Doubters and sceptics spread abroad and thus caused the gradual disappearance of the greatness of that people which had projected from itself the independent personality. It lost its own value, its firm anchor and waited for the "unknown God."

But the unknown God was He who, through His sacrifice, allowed the human personality to develop beyond itself in order that it might find its way back to its origin, with a waking consciousness acquired entirely by effort, after a passage rich in knowledge through the phenomenal world of the senses. Thus there was added to the original forces a newly acquired element, lifted out of deep material density.

And this path was prepared in deep racial seclusion within that folk which developed parallel with Hellenism, and which had the mission of bringing to mankind, in flesh and in truth, the one God, the Ego-God.

After the enslavement and degeneration of the Greek peoples, which followed closely upon the expeditions of Alexander, when the Roman she-wolf in Caesardom celebrated her orgies elevating Caesar, seized by mad ambition, to Godhood, building altars to him, and forcing her subjects to worship him, something occurred in the seclusion of a distant people which, through its impulse, rescued mankind, saved humanity from brutalization, namely, the sacrificial act of Golgotha. It shattered the might of the Roman she-wolf, that symbol of the life of instinct and force. Rome sank beneath it. New peoples overran the degenerate empire. A new folk-substance absorbed what later led to a new soul-configuration for mankind.

But the spiritually new became interspersed with the concretions from what had exhausted itself as a realm of power in the Roman Empire. This imbued the new, tender, spiritual estate with the essence of might and passion which had taken possession of the forms ultimately prevailing there. These forms were, to a great extent, taken over together with the already decadent spirit which had permeated them and the germ of disintegration which should have been overcome, but was not.

The phases of this struggle between the new and the remains of the ancient spirituality which had been taken over form the history of the Middle Ages and of the New Age. These can be traced in the development of the church, in the secret brotherhoods, in the orders of the Monks and Knights, in the so-called heretical confraternities, in the humanistic stream, in the Reformation.

Then came the new natural philosophy, natural science, the mechanistic interpretations of the universe, the limits to knowledge, Ignorabimus. In philosophy, a barren subjectivity, a severance from the whole of the cosmos, a subjective idea of the individual—the whole rich phenomenal world; a psychology without knowledge of the soul and spirit, yes, even denying them. Here matter became the point of departure for researches into soul and spirit.

Matter was victorious in all directions and a spiritual chaos began which reached its climax in our own time, drawing mankind into its vortex until that world catastrophe was reached within the effect of which we are still living. We have reached this point in human history and our enlightened minds are prophesying the downfall of the Occident.

In this world of encompassing darkness, there shines a source of light. It has been revealed to us by a man who towered immeasurably above his time. This source pours light upon that event which occurred in human evolution for mankind's salvation at a time when the Roman delirium was casting the world into chains. It brings us what we need in order that the central point of human and earthly happenings may again be understood, that belief may be changed into knowledge, unbelief into understanding. It is active among us since the beginning of this dark century with those forces which are able to transform our darkness into spiritual light.

This source of light revealed itself to those of us who were seeking the path to the lost mysteries. An Initiate was present who could be the guide. He led us, urging us on without ceasing, first with reserve, then in wisdom and insight as the need of the time demanded. We had not grown up to what we received, but we listened, collected and wrote it down, knowing that a time would come when we should have to hand on to others what had been so bounteously given to us, a time which would make grateful acknowledgment to us for it. It is this that a humanity, matured in sorrow and affliction, needs for its salvation and its advancement. The moment has come for us to fulfill this task, therefore we must no longer hold back.

Rudolf Steiner has again paved the way to the Christ for the world. He laid his hand on the wheel of human evolution which was rushing along into the abyss and checked it. He alone resisted the forces of descent, pulled back the wheel with a strong hand and guided it again toward the slow ascent. It was slow, for the band that surrounded him was small and the greatness of what he had to give fairly overwhelmed it. If the humanity of our day had had organs sufficiently capable of receiving what he gave, a new era would have dawned with infinite, impelling force and sun-soaring eagle flight. But what was capable of awakening the slumbering human organs had to occur gradually through hard labour. Through uninterrupted effort, collecting stone by stone, Rudolf Steiner built the foundation for an understanding of the facts about the world and humanity which became continually more subtle, for the construction of concepts of ever increasing fineness. Never in a public lecture did he shrink back from building this foundation anew. Then gradually, where he had his constantly returning audience, he proceeded a step further on the path which leads to healthy, spiritual knowledge. Never did he permit himself to toss off anything that had any semblance of the sensational; never did he wish to overpower a human soul. Each lecture was something that sprang up organically, that sank its roots deep in the soil, drawing up the forces of the earth, dipping down into the colour-shimmer of the surging ether-worlds, into the quickening spirituality, but permitting the luminous corolla of the resulting new concepts to emerge through inner necessity from the well-constructed conceptual organism. A growing, creative, active force—each thought-structure—and a living work of art! One stood amazed before the perfection of this thought-structure, but one remained free in relation to it astonished at the immensity and beauty of what thus arose before the inner eye with a luminous necessity.

Then about the turn of the century there came considerable chaotic activity rustling and bustling upon our materialistic culture, ghostly tappings out of the border lands of the spiritual world. It took courage, endless courage and karmic necessity to bring order into all this disorder and thereby call odium upon himself; to face the accusation that he was anachronistically immersed in neo-oriental streams.

But destiny stood challenging at the threshold of the 20th century, demanding the most vigorous action, namely, the conquest of the dragon of materialism which held our world firmly encircled, threatening to crush it in its embrace. The very structure of the earth, believed to be so solid, soon shook, as the world and civil wars gave eloquent and gruesome evidence.

Alongside, in helpful goodness, with his deep-seeing glance, stood the bearer of the spirit who seemed to have gathered all the riddles of earthly difficulties and of earthly suffering and to have reflected back in quiet restfulness all the splendour of the spiritual world. He knew that he had to illuminate and make this earthly darkness glow with Golden Wisdom, until a heightened consciousness had awakened within mankind. The task was fulfilled. Golden Wisdom, drawn down from the Christ-Spirit-Sun and given to us, is present here acting among many. It penetrates our earth and its heavy, dense, materialistic world of thought.

By drawing down supersensible knowledge and perceptions into our world of concepts and thoughts, by transforming them into thought-forms which were able to energize our conscious activity, through this fine alchemy, a new soul-substance has been created which can have a vitalizing effect upon our deadened spiritual organs. The force for this revitalization streams out of the Mystery of Golgotha, but there must be a human activity springing up to meet it, understanding how to open itself up to it. In order that this might occur, Rudolf Steiner was active among us. All that he did, wrote, thought, served this one purpose to make our conceptual and sentient world so alive that it might open itself up again, with strength, to the Christ and thus activate our life of will, so that it might actually join itself with Him.

An immense life-work lies before us dedicated to this one goal which is a comprehension, a synthesis of those other aims, namely, the reunion and reciprocal penetration of the three realms of science, art, and religion, formerly working in harmony, now divided; the comprehension of the spiritual meaning concealed in the ideals of liberty, equality, and fraternity; the awakening of the human ego to a full consciousness of itself and its cosmic membership. All these aims are to be attained only through the strengthening of the human being with the Christ-Impulse.

The whole of cosmic wisdom must be called into play in order to understand this greatest of all mysteries. The other mysteries were a preparation for this, and Rudolf Steiner led us gradually and steadily into their essence and meaning. They had all pointed to what took place on Golgotha. Step by step he brought us nearer to this understanding. Cosmogony, theogony, geography, knowledge of man and science, already flowering in the thought-life of mankind, supplied building stones.

But there are critics of various kinds who announce what fits into their party program. There are also those among them, men of prominence, who boldly affirm, because it suits them to do so, that although there is much to be recognized in Rudolf Steiner's genius, still one must turn away from him because he rejects the Christ. But those who took the trouble to study Rudolf Steiner's work before commenting upon it found it otherwise. They soon saw how it could become helpful to them.

A number of theologians came to Rudolf Steiner and said to him:— Our churches are deserted; our seminars do not give us what we can hand on to hungry souls as the bread of life! You alone have the power to help us. Will you give us something that will make it possible for us to help others inside our parish activities? Otherwise, we must renounce the vocation of priesthood. And Rudolf Steiner gave them what they requested, that is, he gave them the key to the gospels, the living Christ, the Word that leads to the rite of Consecration.

He said to them: You have asked me for something that you can give to those who are not yet strong enough to achieve spiritual science and spiritual communion through their own efforts. You wish to guide them on the path to the sources of that knowledge which awakens men, makes them free and fully conscious in accordance with the demands of the time. You may help in the work in this way if your activity does not become self-interest; if your thought for the church does not prevail over that for the spirit; if the path of the ministry gradually leads to a strengthening of the human ego so that it may in freedom and awareness unite itself with the divine world and the heart of Christ that shines in the sun and pulses through the earth. You have wished it and have promised it; act accordingly, and remain true to your words.

They went away and founded the *Fellowship for a Christian Regeneration* for the salvation of many souls. In this fellowship knowledge of the Gospels, to which Rudolf Steiner gave the key, is earnestly pursued.

He had begun with this even in the earliest years of his activities in Spiritual Science by always introducing into his lectures something that led us to the Tree of the Cross and to its meaning as the Tree of Life. At that time his listeners came to him and requested a connected cycle of lectures on the Gospel of St. John. It was granted them. These lectures from the year 1908 we possess in an unfortunately quite incomplete copy. They have been so often asked for and copies have been made in so many places, that we do not wish to withhold them any longer because of their incompleteness. The subject matter will triumph over the incomplete renderings. A breath from the world out of which they have their source still hovers over them. Mankind needs it and needs this subject matter.

The publication of the lectures concerning the other gospels will soon follow this Gospel of St. John. When this introduction into the esoteric gospel was given to us at Whitsuntide, 1908, in Hamburg,—after a similar cycle had for the first time been given in Basel—something like a Pentecostal fire and the wafting of a Galilean springtime passed through our souls. Whitsuntide again approaches, accompanying the appearance of this book. May this be a favorable omen for the book.

Whitsuntide is the festival of the Holy Spirit which is active within human hearts. May the Spirit which rules in this book find its way to the souls of men who thirst after truth and are of good will.

I

THE DOCTRINE OF THE LOGOS

Our lectures[1] upon the Gospel of St. John will have a double purpose. One will be the deepening of the concepts of Spiritual Science themselves and their expansion in many directions, and the other will be to make this great document itself comprehensible by means of the thoughts that will arise in our souls in consequence of these deepened and expanded concepts. I beg you to hold clearly in mind that it is the intention of these lectures to proceed in these two directions. It should not be simply a question of explanations *of* this Gospel, but rather that by means of the latter we shall penetrate into the deep mysteries of existence and we should hold very clearly in mind how the perceptive method of Spiritual Science must be developed when we are dealing with any of the great historical records handed down to us by the different religions of the world. In fact we might imagine that if the exponent of Spiritual Science speaks about the Gospel of St. John, he will do so just as others have often done, that is, he will take some such document as this Gospel as a basis in order that he may draw from it the truths that are under discussion and present them on the authority of this religious document. But this can never be the concern of a spiritually scientific, cosmic point of view. It must be a quite different one. If Spiritual Science is to fulfill its true mission in respect of the modern human spirit, then it should point out that if men will only learn to use their inner forces and capacities—their forces and capacities of spiritual perception—they will be able, by applying them, to penetrate into the mysteries of life, into what is concealed within the spiritual worlds behind the world of the senses. The fact that men can penetrate to the mysteries of life through the use of inner capacities, that they are able to reach the creative forces and beings of the universe through their own cognition must be brought more and more into the consciousness of present day humanity. Thus it becomes evident that a knowledge of the mystery of this Gospel can be gained by men,

---

[1] The reader will please remember that he is reading a lecture, something given by the spoken word, hence very different from the written word. The lecturer was speaking to students and had often to repeat. He was moreover never able to correct the stenogram. Ed.

independent of every tradition, independent of every historical document.

In order to make this absolutely clear, we shall have to express ourselves in quite radical terms. Let us suppose that through some circumstance all religious records had been lost, and that men possessed only those capacities which they have today; they should, nevertheless, be able to penetrate into life's mysteries, if they only retain those capacities. They should be able to reach the divine-spiritual creating forces and beings which lie concealed behind the physical world. And Spiritual Science must depend entirely upon these independent sources of knowledge, irrespective of all records. However, after having investigated the divine-spiritual mysteries of the world independently, we can then take up the actual religious documents themselves. Only then can we recognize their true worth, for we are, in a certain sense, free and independent of them. What has previously been independently discovered is now recognized within the documents themselves. And you may be sure that for anyone who has pursued this path, these writings will suffer no diminution in value, no lessening of the respect and veneration due them.

Let us make this point quite clear by means of a comparison with something very different. It is true that Euclid, the old geometrician, first gave us that geometry which every school boy today studies at a certain stage of his school life. But is the acquisition of a knowledge of geometry absolutely dependent upon this book of Euclid? I ask you, how many pupils today study elementary geometry without knowing the least thing about this first book in which Euclid presented the most rudimentary geometrical facts? They study these geometrical facts quite apart from this Euclidian book, because geometry originates in a capacity of the human spirit. If the pupil has first studied geometry by means of his own spiritual faculty, and afterwards takes up the great work by Euclid, he then understands how to appreciate it adequately. For the first time then he finds in it what he has already made into a capacity of his own mind, and he learns to value the form in which the corresponding knowledge was presented for the first time. Thus it is possible today to discover the great cosmic facts presented in the Gospel of St. John by means of the forces slumbering within the human soul without knowing anything about the Gospel itself, just as the pupil acquires a knowledge of geometry without knowing anything about the first book of Euclid.

If previously equipped with knowledge about the higher worlds, we take up this Gospel and inquire into what is disclosed therein concerning the spiritual history of mankind, we find that the deepest mysteries of the spiritual world are concealed within a book, are given to mankind in a book, and because we already know the truths concerning the divine spiritual world, we can now recognize the divine-spiritual nature of this document, this Gospel of St. John. For this is altogether the right way to approach those documents which deal with spiritual things. What is the position of the exponent of Spiritual Science in relation to those researchers of records dealing with spiritual matters who understand very well, from the standpoint of language, everything presented in documents like the Gospel of St. John; in other words what is his position in relation to those who are pure philologists? (Even the theological researchers of a certain type are today only philologists in respect of the content of such books). Let us take once more the parallel of the geometry of Euclid. Will the best expounder of geometry be the one who in his own way can make a good literal translation without the vaguest conception of geometrical knowledge? Something very extraordinary would result were such a person to attempt to translate Euclid, understanding previously nothing at all about geometry. On the other hand, even if the translator himself were a poor philologist, but understood geometry, he would still be able to give the proper value to this book. The exponent of Spiritual Science is in a similar position in relation to many other researchers of the Gospel of St. John. Today this Gospel is often interpreted in much the same way as the philologist would explain the geometry of Euclid. But from Spiritual Science itself we can gain knowledge about the spiritual worlds recorded in this Gospel. So the spiritual scientist stands in the same relation to this spiritual document as the geometrician to Euclid. He has brought with him something which he now is able to discover in the Gospel itself.

We do not need to dwell upon the objection, that in this way much is "read into" the documents. We shall soon see that whoever understands the content of the Gospel of St. John need not put into it something that is not there and if he understands the nature of the Spiritual Science interpretation, he will not need to concern himself much with this reproach. Just as other documents do not depreciate in value or lose in veneration when their true content is known, so too is such the case with this Gospel. To anyone who has penetrated into the mysteries of the world, it becomes one of the most significant documents in the spiritual life of mankind.

If we consider its exact content, we may then ask: Why should the Gospel of St. John, which for the spiritual researcher is such an important document, be pushed more and more into the background in relation to the other Gospels by the very theologians who should be called upon to explain it? We shall touch upon this as a preliminary question before entering upon a consideration of the Gospel itself.

You all know that in respect of this Gospel, extraordinary points of view and opinions have possessed certain minds. In olden times it was revered as one of the deepest and most significant documents in the custody of mankind concerning the being of Christ Jesus and His activities upon earth; and in the earlier periods of Christianity, it would never have entered the mind of any one to consider it other than a powerful, historical testimony of the events in Palestine. But in recent times this has all changed and just those who think they stand most securely upon the foundation of historical research are the ones who have, for the most part, undermined the foundation upon which such a concept rests. For some time, and this can now be reckoned in centuries, men have begun to notice the contradictions present in the Gospels, and after much vacillation, the following has become the accepted view especially among theologians: We find many contradictions in the Gospels and it is impossible to see how it happens that in the four Gospels, from four sides, the events in Palestine are so differently related. When we take the descriptions given according to Matthew, Mark, Luke and John, we have so many different accounts of this or that event that it becomes impossible to believe they are all in agreement with the historical facts. Little by little this became the opinion of those who wished to investigate these things.

In more recent times, the point of view has developed that it is possible to establish a certain harmony between the descriptions of the events in Palestine in the first three Gospels, but that the Gospel of St. John, however, differs greatly in its narrations from the other three. Therefore, in respect of the historical facts, it is preferable that the first three Gospels should be believed, the Gospel of St. John possessing less historical authenticity. Thus gradually the time came when it was stated as a fact that the Gospel of St. John was not written with the same purpose as the first three. The authors of these other Gospels, it was said, wished only to relate what occurred, whereas the writer of the Gospel of St. John did not have this purpose, but quite a different one. And, for various reasons, these critics have yielded to the supposition that the St. John document was written at a comparatively late period,—but we shall speak of these things again. Most of the researchers believe it was not written until the third or fourth decade of the second century A. D.— although perhaps even in the second decade. Therefore they say it was written at a time when Christianity had already become wide-spread in a very definite form and when, perhaps, it already had its enemies. For hostility against Christianity arose from various sources and those who held this opinion said that in the author we have a man before us who endeavoured to present a book of instruction, a kind of apotheosis, or something like a vindication of Christianity in the face of those streams of opposition which had risen up against it. But this writer, they said, never had the intention of picturing accurately the historical facts, his idea being rather to present his own position in relation to his Christ. Thus many see nothing more in this Gospel than a kind of poem imbued with religion, which the author wrote out of a religiously poetical feeling for his Christ, for the purpose of inspiring others also and bringing them into a similar mood. Perhaps this opinion is not expressed everywhere in such extreme terms, but if you study literature, you will find this opinion to be wide-spread, that it has a response in the souls of many of our contemporaries;—indeed, such a belief harmonizes exactly with the sentiments of our contemporaries.

A certain disinclination toward any such idea of an historical beginning as we find depicted in the very first words of the Gospel of St. John has been developing for several centuries among men who have come more and more to a materialistic way of thinking. I should like you just to remember that the very first words permit of no other interpretation than that in Jesus of Nazareth, who lived at the beginning of our Christian era, a being of a very high spiritual order was incarnated. When the author in his wholly characteristic manner spoke of Jesus, he could not do otherwise than begin with what he calls the "Word" or the "Logos" and say: "the Word was in the beginning and all things came into being through It." If we consider the Word in its full significance, we should say that the author of this Gospel felt impelled to speak of the Logos as the origin of the world, the highest to which the human being can lift his spirit, and to say that through the Logos, the First Cause, all things have come into being. Then the writer continues: "The Logos became flesh and dwelt among us." This simply means: "You have seen Him who dwelt among us, but you will only be able to understand Him if you recognize the same Principle dwelling within Him through which everything that is about you in the plant, animal and human kingdoms has come into being." If we do not interpret with too much artificiality, then we must say that according to this document a Principle of the highest order at one time incarnated in human flesh. Let us compare the appeal which such thoughts make to the human heart with the words of many modern theologians. You can read the following in present day theological works and hear it presented in various ways in lectures: We no longer call upon some Supersensible Principle. We prefer the Jesus described in the first three Gospels, for that is the simple Man of Nazareth *who is like other men.*

In a certain sense this has become an ideal for many theologians and an effort is being made to place everything that has become a part of history as much as possible upon the same level as ordinary human events. It disturbs people that any such exalted being as the Christ of the Gospel of St. John should tower above all others. Therefore they speak of the Christ as the Apotheosis of Jesus, "the simple Man of Nazareth" and He appeals to them in this character, because then they can say: "Yes, we have also a Socrates and other great men." To be sure they make him different from these others but still they are using a certain standard for an ordinary humanity when they speak of "the simple Man of Nazareth." This expression "the simple Man of Nazareth," which you can find today in innumerable theological works, also in theological-academic writings in what is called "Liberal Theology," has a very close connection with the materialistic tendency of mankind which has been in process of development now for centuries. According to this "Liberal Theology" there is only a physical sense-world; at least it alone has significance.

But in those periods of human evolution in which humanity could still lift its perceptions to the unseen world, it was possible to say: Of course this or that historical personality outwardly, in external appearance, may be compared with the "simple Man of Nazareth," but in what is spiritual and invisible in His personality, Jesus of Nazareth stands before us as a unique figure. However, when men had lost their insight into the supersensible and invisible world, then the standard for a humanity above the average was also lost and this is especially noticeable in the religious conceptions of life. Let us have no illusions! Materialism first forced its way into the religious life. Materialism in its relation to the facts of outer natural science is very, very much less dangerous for the spiritual development of mankind than it is in its relation to the interpretation of religious mysteries.

As an illustration, let us consider the true spiritual interpretation of the Last Supper, the changing of Bread and Wine into Flesh and Blood and we shall see that the Last Supper loses nothing in value and importance through this spiritual interpretation. It will be a spiritual interpretation about which we are to hear. This was also the early Christian conception when there was still far more spiritual understanding among men than there is today, and it was still current in the first half of the Middle Ages when many could comprehend the words, "This is my Body, this is my Blood," as we shall here learn to understand them. However, in the course of centuries, this spiritual interpretation was necessarily lost. We shall learn the reason why.

In the Middle Ages there existed a very extraordinary current which streamed more deeply through the souls of men than is possible to believe, for we learn very little from present-day history about the way human souls were gradually evolved and what they have experienced. About the second half of the Middle Ages we find a deep current of thought flowing through the Christian minds of Europe, for it was then that the earlier spiritual interpretation of the doctrine of the Last Supper was authoritatively changed into a materialistic one. In these words, "This is my Body, this is my Blood," men could only imagine a material process, a physical transubstantiation of bread and wine into flesh and blood. What was formerly conceived in a spiritual sense began to assume a grossly materialistic meaning. Here materialism crept into the religious life long before it seized upon natural science.

Another illustration is no less significant. We must not imagine that in any of the authoritative explanations of the Middle Ages concerning the Story of Creation, the six days of Creation were interpreted to mean days of twenty-four hours, such as we have today. This interpretation would never have entered the minds of any of the leading theological teachers, because they understood what was presented in these documents. They still knew how to attach a meaning to the words of the Bible. Has it any meaning whatsoever in discussing these documents about the creation, to speak in our present manner of days of creation twenty-four hours long? What is the meaning of a day? A day is what results from the mutual relationship between the rotating earth and the sun. We can only speak of days in our sense when we think of the relationship between the sun and the earth with its movement as it is at the present time. But we find in the Book of Genesis the first narration of any such mutual relationship between sun and earth in connection with the fourth period, the fourth "day" of creation. Therefore "days" in our sense could not possibly have had their beginning prior to the fourth day of the history of creation. Before that time it would have been foolish to imagine days as we have them now. Since only on the fourth "day" conditions arose which made day and night possible, one cannot speak of days in the present sense before that. Then came a time when men no longer recognized the spiritual significance of the words day and night, when they were of the opinion that the only kind of time possible was what they knew in connection with physical days. So to the materialistically minded man and even to the theologian, a day of creation also meant a day like our present day, because they knew of no other.

The older theologians spoke differently about these things. Such an one would have said, first and foremost, that nothing non-essential was to be found in important passages in the old religious documents. To illustrate this, let us consider one special passage. Let us take the twenty-first verse of the second chapter of the First Book of Moses. There we read: "Then the Lord God caused a deep sleep to fall upon the human creature, and he slept." The earlier commentators laid very special importance upon this passage. Those who have understood a little of the evolution of the spiritual forces and capacities of mankind know that there are different states of consciousness, that what we call sleep in the average man is only a transitory state which in the future will develop into one in which the human being, independent of the body, will perceive the spiritual world. (This is today already the case with the initiates.) Therefore the commentators said: God permitted Adam to fall into a deep sleep and then he could perceive what he could not otherwise perceive with the physical sense-organs. This means a clairvoyant sleep—and what is related here is the experience of a higher state of consciousness. So Adam fell into a deep sleep. This was an old interpretation and it was said that a religious document would not have spoken of God's permitting a deep sleep to fall upon the human being if, at an earlier time, he had already gone through such an experience. We are thereby shown that this is the first sleep and that before this time the human being was in states of consciousness in which he was still able constantly to perceive spiritual things. This is what was related to the people.

Today it is our purpose to show that there were, at one time, wholly spiritual interpretations of Biblical documents and that when the materialistic tendency arose, it read into the Bible what is now objected to by liberal-minded people. The materialistically inclined mind first created what it then itself later opposed. So you see how in fact the materialistic tendency in mankind arose and how, because of it, the real, true understanding of religious documents has been lost. If Spiritual Science performs its task and points out what mysteries lie hidden behind physical life, then it will be seen that these very mysteries have been described in the religious documents themselves. The outer trivial materialism which is today considered so dangerous, is only the last phase of the materialism I have described to you. The Bible was first materialistically interpreted. Had this never been done, a Haeckel would never have interpreted nature materialistically in an outer physical science. What was sown as a seed in the realm of religion in the 14th and 15th centuries came to fruition in the 19th in natural science. This brought with it the impossibility of reaching any understanding of the Gospel of St. John except by penetrating into its spiritual foundations. If it is not understood, it will certainly be underrated. Because those who no longer understood it were sickened by a materialistic mode of thought, it appeared to them in the light described above.

A very simple comparison will explain how this Gospel differs from the other three. Let us imagine a mountain and on the mountain and mountain slopes at certain levels, four men are standing and these men—let us say three of them—sketch what they see below. Each of them will make a different sketch according to the position at which he stands, but of course each one of the three pictures is true from its own standpoint. The fourth man, who stands above on the very summit and sketches what is below, will perceive and draw yet another view. Thus it is with the point of view of the three evangelists, the synoptists—Matthew, Mark and Luke—in contrast to that of the evangelist John, who merely describes the facts from another standpoint. And to what lengths have learned interpreters not gone in order to make the Gospel of St. John comprehensible! Often one must really marvel at exact researchers' explanations of what would so easily be seen through were our age not one of the greatest possible belief in authority. Belief in an infallible science has today reached its highest point.

Thus the very prologue to this Gospel becomes something very difficult for the theologians imbued with materialism. The teaching about the Logos, or the Word, has caused great difficulties, for they say: We should have liked so much to have everything plain and simple and naive, then along comes the Gospel of St. John speaking of such lofty philosophical things, of the Logos, of Life, of Light! Philologists are always accustomed to ask about the origin of a thing. With the writings of recent times it is the same. Read what is written about Goethe's Faust. Everywhere you find pointed out the origin of this or that motive. Thus books hundreds of years old have been ferreted out in order to discover, for example, the origin of the word "Worm," employed by Goethe. In the same way the question is also asked, where did the Evangelist John get the idea of the "Logos?" The other Evangelists who spoke to the simple, plain human understanding did not express themselves in such a personal way. It was said further that the author of this Gospel was a man of Greek education, and then it was pointed out that in Philo of Alexandria, the Greeks have a writer who also speaks of the "Logos." So it was thought that in cultured Grecian circles one spoke of the Logos when wishing to speak of something exalted, and that it was from this source that St. John derived this word. This again was considered as a proof that the writer of the Gospel of St. John did not rely upon the same traditions as the writers of the other Gospels, but that influenced by

Greek culture, he re-coined the facts in accordance with it. Thus, it is alleged, the very first words of the Gospel, "In the beginning was the Word, and the Word was with God and the Word was a God" show that the Logos-idea of Philo had entered into the spirit of the writer of this Gospel and had influenced his form of presentation.

The attention of such people should be called to the very first words of the Gospel of St. Luke:—"Forasmuch as many have undertaken to speak of those events which have thus happened amongst us, even as they have been transmitted unto us by those who from the beginning were eye-witnesses and ministers of the *Word* (*Logos*), it seemed well to me also, having examined with diligence all things as they were from the beginning, to relate them unto thee, most excellent Theophilus."

Here at the very beginning we read that what he is about to relate is what had been transmitted by those who have been eye-witnesses and ministers of the "Word." It is extraordinary that St. John should have received this from his Greek culture and that St. Luke, who according to this view belonged to the simple folk, also speaks of the "Logos" without this culture. Such things should call the attention of even believers in authority to the fact that arguments which lead to such conclusions are really not exact ones, but only prejudices; (it is the materialistic spectacles that have brought out this idea of the Gospel of St. John). They should call attention also to the fact that the St. John document should be placed alongside the other Gospels in the manner just characterized, because in the Gospel of St. Luke the Logos is also spoken of. What was said by those who were eye-witnesses and ministers of the Logos shows that in olden times the Logos was spoken of as something which the people knew about and with which they were familiar. And this we must particularly hold in mind in order that we may penetrate more deeply into the first paradigmatic verses of the Gospel of St. John. What was a writer speaking about, if at that time he used the word "Logos" or "Word" in our sense? What could he have meant?

You will not come to this ancient conception of the "Logos" through theoretical interpretations and abstract intellectual discussions, but you must enter in spirit into the entire feeling-life of all those who have spoken in this way about the "Logos." These people also observed the things about them; but it is not sufficient that we simply observe what is in our environment, the important thing is that the feelings of our hearts and souls should also participate in what we observe. We should consider a thing of greater or less importance according to what we are able to discern in it. We all observe the kingdoms of nature about us, the minerals, plants, animals and man. We call the human kingdom the most perfect creation, the mineral the most imperfect. Within the respective kingdoms of nature we differentiate again beings of higher and lower grades. Men have experienced this quite differently in different ages. Those who spoke from the standpoint of the Gospel of St. John found one thing above all else to be of very great importance. They looked down upon the lower animal kingdom and let their glance sweep up as far as man and in this evolutionary sweep they traced something very definite. They said: There is one quality which shows most profoundly the superiority of the higher beings over the lower. This is the capacity to utter aloud in words what exists within the soul, to communicate thoughts to the surrounding world by means of words. Behold the lower animals! They are mute, they do not express their pain and pleasure. They squeak or make other sounds, but it is the outer scraping and rubbing of the physical organs which produce these sounds, as in the case of the lobster. The higher we go in evolution, the more do we see the capacity developed for expressing the inner feelings in sound and communicating in tones the experiences of the soul. Therefore, they said, the human being stands thus high above other creatures, because not only can he express his pleasure and pain in words, but because he is able to put into words what rises above the personal, that is to say, the spiritual, the impersonal, and to express this by means of thoughts.

And there were among the followers of the Logos-doctrine those who said that there existed a period prior to the time when man had developed his present form, a form in which it is now possible for him to express in words the most intimate experiences of his soul. It has taken a long time for our earth to evolve to its present form. (We shall hear later how this earth came into existence.) But if we examine the earlier states of the earth, we do not yet find mankind in its present shape, nor do we find any creature which could utter aloud what it was experiencing inwardly. Our world began with mute creatures and only by degrees did beings appear upon this dwelling place of ours who could express aloud their innermost experiences through having acquired a command of language.

The followers of St. John said further: What appears last in the human being existed in the world in the very earliest times. We fancy that the human being in his present form did not exist in the earlier conditions of the earth. But in an imperfect, mute form he was there and little by little he evolved into a being endowed with the Logos or the Word. This became possible through the fact that what appears within him later as the creative principle was there from the very beginning, in a higher reality. What struggled forth out of the soul was in the beginning the divine creative principle. The Word, which sounds forth from the soul, the Logos, was there in the beginning and so guided evolution that at last a being came into existence, in whom it also could manifest. What finally appears in time and space was already there in spirit from the beginning.

In order that this may be quite clear, let us make the following analogy. I have here a flower before me. This corolla, these petals, what were they a short time ago? A little seed. And in the seed, this white flower existed in potentiality. Were it not there potentially, this flower could not have come into existence. And whence comes the seed? It springs again from just such a flower. The blossom precedes the seed or fruit and again in like manner, the seed, from which this blossom has sprung, has been evolved out of a similar plant.

Thus these followers of the Logos-doctrine observed the human being and said: If we go back in evolution, we find him in earlier conditions still mute, still incapable of speech. But just as the seed came from the blossom, so likewise the mute human-seed in the beginning had its origin in a God endowed with the power of uttering the "Word." The lily-of-the-valley produces the seed and the seed again the lily-of-the-valley; in like manner the divine creative Word created the mute human seed—and when this primeval creative Word had glided into the human seed, in order to spring up again within it, it sounded forth in words. When we go back in human evolution we meet an imperfect human being and the significance of evolution is, that finally the Logos or Word which discloses the depths of the human soul may appear as its flower. In the beginning this mute human being appears as seed of the Logos-endowed human being, but, on the other hand, has sprung from the Logos-endowed God. The human being has sprung from a mute human creature, not gifted with speech, but: *In the beginning was the Logos, the Word.*

Thus those who understand the Logos-doctrine in its earlier significance press forward to the divine creative Word which is the beginning of existence and to which the writer of the Gospel of St. John refers. Let us hear what he says in the very first words:—"In the beginning was the Word and the Word was with God and the Word was a God."

They will ask where is the "Word" today? The Word is also here today and the Word is with men and the Word has become man! Thus the writer of the Gospel of St. John forges a link between man and God and indeed we find sounding forth in the beginning of this Gospel a doctrine easy for every human heart to understand.

In this introductory lecture today, I wished to picture to you in simple words—but more from the standpoint of feeling and of inward sensing—how originally a believer in the doctrine of the Logos interpreted these words of the Gospel of St. John. And after having entered into the soul-mood which existed when these words were first heard, we shall be that much better able to penetrate into the deep meaning which lies at the foundation of this Gospel.

Further, we shall see that what we call Spiritual Science is in fact a restitution of the Gospel of St. John and that it puts us in the position of being able thoroughly to understand it.

II

ESOTERIC CHRISTIANITY

The first words of the Gospel of St. John touch, in fact, upon the deepest mysteries of the world. This can be seen when we allow the truths of Spiritual Science which lie at their very foundation to pass before our souls. And we must dip deeply into spiritual knowledge, if these first words of this Gospel are to appear to us in the right light. We must recall to memory much that is well known to those of you who for a long time have been occupying yourselves with the Anthroposophical world conception. But today we shall need to expand certain elementary truths of this conception by penetrating further into various significant cosmic mysteries. We need but briefly call to mind how the human being appears to us between the time of waking in the morning and the evening, when he again sinks into sleep. We know that he is composed of a physical body, an ether or life body, an astral body, and an ego. These four members of the human being, however, are in close relationship only during the waking state. It is quite necessary that we remember that during the night, while sleeping, the human creature is, in reality, entirely different from the same creature during the day, during waking day consciousness, for then his four members are assembled in a very different manner. When he sleeps, the physical and ether bodies lie in bed. The astral body and ego, in a certain sense, are loosened from their connections with the physical and ether bodies and are in fact outside of them—we must understand the word *outside* in a spiritual, not in a purely spatial sense. Therefore during the night the human being is a creature consisting of two parts, one that remains lying in bed and another part which separates from the physical and ether bodies. Now we must first of all clearly understand that if, during the night, from the moment of going to sleep to the moment of waking again in the morning, the physical and ether bodies lying in bed were completely abandoned by what fills them throughout the day—that is, the astral body and ego—they could not then exist at all by themselves.

Here at this point we must enter a little more deeply into the cosmic mysteries. When we have the human physical body here before us, we should clearly understand that behind what we can see with the eyes and touch with our hands there is a long evolutionary process. It has passed through this process of evolution in the course of the entire development of our earthly planet. To those of you who have concerned yourselves a little with this subject, it is already well known that our earth has passed through previous states of existence and just as the human being has gone from one incarnation to another or, in other words, has passed through repeated earth lives, so too has the earth passed through other life-states before it reached the condition in which we find it today. There are previous incarnations of a planet just as there are previous incarnations of a human being. Everything in the great world and in the small world is subject to the law of repeated incarnations, and before the earth finally became this earth of ours it had passed through a condition of being which we call the "Ancient *Moon," so called because the present moon contains a portion of that ancient planet. So when we speak of the "Ancient Moon," we do not at all mean the present moon, but a planet similar to the present earth in its earliest stages. Now, just as there is a period between one incarnation and a new birth in the case of human beings, so also is there a period between the incarnation of this planet of ours which we call the Earth, and that one we designate as the Ancient Moon, and the same is true of that life-condition which we call the "Sun." A state which we call the "Sun" preceded the Moon-state of our planet and again this Sun-state was preceded by a "Saturn" life-condition. Thus we can look back on three earlier incarnations of our planet but not as it is today.

Our physical human body received its very first rudiments upon the ancient Saturn. Upon that ancient planet the very first germ of a physical body was at that time created, but, of course, one very different from the human body of the present. Besides the physical body, nothing that is a part of the human being of today was present on ancient Saturn. Only when Saturn was transformed into the Sun, that is to say, during the second incarnation of our Earth-planet, was the ether body added to the

---

* The words Saturn, Sun, Moon, Earth, Jupiter, Venus, and Vulcan when spelt with an initial capital refer to the great cosmic evolutionary periods called "man-bearing periods." The words earth, moon, and sun, spelt with small letters refer to the planets of our present solar system. Ed.

physical body, penetrating and impregnating it. And what was the result? The physical human body underwent a transformation, acquired another form and attained a very different state of existence. During the Sun incarnation of our Earth, the physical body stood at a second stage of its development. But how did it reach this second stage? By becoming an inwardly living body on the Sun, while on Saturn it was still machine-like and automatic. The ether body, which had slipped in, transformed the physical body. Then on the Moon, the astral body slipped into this union of physical and ether bodies. Thus the physical body was again transformed a third time and the ether body a second time. At last upon the Earth, the ego was added to the physical, ether and astral bodies and having now entered into this threefold union, the ego transformed this physical body again, so that at last it became the complicated structure which it is today. Therefore, what you have before you now as the human physical body is a many times transformed entity, and just because it has passed through four stages of evolution it has its present complicated appearance.

If we say, when speaking of our present physical body, that it is composed of the same physical and chemical substances and forces to be found in the minerals out in the cosmos, it must, nevertheless, be quite clear to us that there is an enormous difference between this physical human body and the mineral. Speaking in very elementary terms, we emphasize the difference between the physical human body and the physical body of a mineral—for example, of a rock crystal—when we say that the rock crystal retains its form unless shattered from without. The human physical body, on the contrary, cannot of itself retain its form. It has its form only because and as long as there are within it an ether body, an astral body, and an ego. The moment the ether body, the astral body, and the ego are separated from it, it becomes something quite different from what it is between birth and death; it follows the laws of the physical and chemical substances and forces and decays, while on the other hand the physical body of the mineral remains unchanged.

Something similar is the case with the ether body. Immediately after death the ether and astral bodies and the ego separate from the physical body; then after a time the ether body also leaves this union of astral body and ego and resolves itself into the cosmic ether, just as the physical body disintegrates and goes back into the earth kingdom. There remains behind only that extract of the ether body of which we have often spoken. This remains united with the human being. Therefore we may say that the physical human body is in a certain sense of the same nature as the mineral kingdom about us, nevertheless, we must keep in mind the great difference which exists between the mineral kingdom and the physical human body.

One might say:—Indeed, but you have just stated that on Saturn our physical body was not yet permeated by an ether body, an astral body and an ego, for they were only added on the Sun, Moon and Earth. Therefore at that time, in fact—one might say—the physical body had the character of a mineral. That is true, but we have mentioned three metamorphoses of this physical body that one after the other have succeeded that early life-state of the Saturn period. Even the present mineral, which you have before you as a dead mineral, cannot possibly exist with only a physical body. Let us make it very clear that what has been said and must be repeated is true, that as far as the physical world is concerned, the mineral has only a physical body. Here in the physical world the mineral has only a physical body—however, that is not *literally* true. Just as the physical human body, standing before us, has within it its etheric and astral bodies and its ego which belong to it, so too has the mineral not only a physical body, but also an ether and an astral body, and an ego, however, these higher members of its being are to be found only in higher realms. The mineral has an ether body, but it is to be found in the so-called astral world; it has also an astral body, but it is in the so-called devachanic or heaven-world, and it has an ego, but this exists in a still higher spiritual world. Thus the physical human body differs from the physical body of a mineral in having here in this physical world, in a waking state, its ether and astral bodies and ego within it, while the mineral has not. We know that besides our world there are still other worlds. The world which we ordinarily perceive with our physical senses is permeated by the astral world and this again by the devachanic world which consists of an inferior and a superior region.

In comparison with the mineral, the human being is an especially favored creature, because during waking-consciousness he has his other three members within him. The mineral does not contain these members within itself, so we must think of it as not existing wholly upon the physical plane. Think of a human finger-nail. You will concede that nowhere outside in Nature can you find this finger-nail existing as an independent entity, for if it is to grow, it presupposes the rest of the human organism— it cannot exist without this. Now imagine a tiny creature with eyes that can see only your finger-nail, but has no capacity to see the rest of your organism. Such a tiny creature would look out into the rest of space, but would see nothing besides your finger-nail. Thus the minerals on the physical plane are like the finger-nail and you only perceive them in their entirety when you rise into higher realms. There they have their ether and astral bodies and egos and here only their physical member. All this we must hold firmly in mind in order that it may be quite clear that in a higher reality there can be no entity that does not possess some kind of ether and astral body and ego. A purely physical being can have no existence; to exist at all it must have an ether and an astral body, and an ego.

However, in all that has been said today there is in fact a certain contradiction. We have stated that the human being, in the night while asleep, is entirely different from the creature we see during the day when he is awake. By day he is quite comprehensible to us; we have him there before us as a four-fold being. But now let us approach him in sleep and observe his physical nature. Here we have the physical body and the ether body lying in bed—the astral body and ego outside. Thus arises the contradictory condition of having before us a being deserted by its astral body and ego. The stone does not sleep. Its ether and astral bodies and ego do not penetrate it, but remain constantly in the same relationship with it. With the human being, on the contrary, the astral body and ego depart each night and he does not concern himself about his physical and ether bodies, but leaves them to themselves. This fact is not always fully considered. Every night the human being, in his truly spiritual part, takes leave of his physical and ether bodies which he himself deserts. However, these bodies would not be able to exist by themselves, because no physical body, and for that matter no ether body, can exist by itself. Even the stone must be permeated by its higher members. Therefore you can easily comprehend that it is wholly impossible for your physical body and ether body to remain in bed at night without an astral body and ego. What occurs then during the night? Your own astral body and ego are indeed not within the physical and ether bodies, but present in their place there is another ego and another astral body. At this point, occultism calls your attention to a divine-spiritual existence and to higher spiritual powers. During the night, while your own ego and astral body are outside your physical and ether bodies, the astral body and ego of higher, divine-spiritual powers are actually active within them. And the reason for this is the following:

When we consider the whole of human evolution from the Saturn stage through the Sun and Moon periods as far as the Earth, we might indeed say that upon Saturn only the physical human body existed, that there was no human ether body, no human astral body and no human ego within this physical body. But this physical body, at that time, could have no more existed by itself than the stone today can exist by itself. The physical body of that time could only exist because it was permeated by the ether and astral bodies and the ego of divine-spiritual beings which dwelt within it, and they still dwell there today. Then on the Sun, when our own ether body entered into this physical body, the smaller human ether body amalgamated, as it were, with the earlier ether body of divine-spiritual powers. Even upon Saturn the physical body was permeated by divine-spiritual beings.

If we have now understood this properly, we come to a deeper comprehension of the present human being and we are in a position to repeat and to understand better what has been taught in Esoteric Christianity from the beginning. This Esoteric Christianity has always been fostered alongside the outer Christian exoteric teaching. I have often pointed out that Paul, the great apostle of Christianity, used his powerful, fiery gift of eloquence to teach Christianity to the people, but that at the same time he founded an esoteric school, the director of which was Dionysius, the Areopagite, mentioned in the Acts of the Apostles. In this Christian Esoteric School at Athens which was directly founded by Paul himself, the purest Spiritual Science was taught. And now, having brought together the necessary material in the above observations, we shall be able to place before our souls what was taught there.

This school also taught that when we observe the human being standing before us in his waking state, we find him composed of physical body, ether body, astral body, and ego. It is of little importance that the names used were not exactly the same as those used today. Even at that time the stage of evolution at which humanity now stands was already predicated. This human being, consisting of these four members, has not always been as he now appears to us. If we wish to observe him composed of these four members only, then we must not observe him as he is today, but we must retrace our evolutionary steps back to the Lemurian period. It was at that time that the ego became united with the human being composed of physical, ether, and astral bodies. Thus one might truly say that then, in the real sense of the word, the human being consisted of physical, ether, and astral bodies, and ego.

But since that time every human being has passed through many incarnations. What then is the significance of this evolution by means of incarnations? It is that from incarnation to incarnation the ego works upon and transforms the three members of its being. It begins by first transforming its astral body. In the average man of today the astral body is not just as it was in the first earthly incarnation before the ego had worked upon it. In the first incarnation upon the earth the ego, working from within outwardly, transformed certain thoughts, feelings, and passions which originally had been given to men, and from incarnation to incarnation these were changed more and more through the activity of the ego. Thus it may be said that the human being has today not only the four members, physical, ether, and astral bodies, and ego, but through the activity of the ego within the astral body, he has now a member which is the actual creation of the ego itself. In each human being of today, the astral body is two-fold; it has one part that has been transformed by the ego, and another part not so transformed. This will continue and a time will come for every human being when his entire astral body will become a creation of his ego. It is the custom in oriental wisdom to call that part of the astral body, which has already been transformed by the ego, by the name of Manas; in English, Spirit-Self. Although the human being is still composed of his four members, we can now distinguish five parts: physical, ether, and astral bodies, and ego; and as fifth member, the transformed part of the astral body, Manas or Spirit-Self. Thus we may say that in every human being the astral body contains within it Manas or Spirit-Self, the work of the ego, the product of the activity of the ego.

The human being will continue to work upon himself. The Earth will pass through further incarnations and humanity will acquire by degrees the capacity—which today can be acquired by the initiate—of working also upon the ether body. It is true the average man today is already working upon his ether body and that part of it which is transformed into a product of the ego is called Budhi or Life-Spirit. He will finally reach the point where, by means of his ego, he will transform his physical body also. That part of the physical body which is transformed by the ego is called Atman or Spirit-Man.

Let us allow our glance to sweep to the far distant future after the Earth has passed through other planetary forms, other incarnations, after —as occultism describes it—it has gone through the Jupiter, Venus, and Vulcan states of existence. The human being will then stand upon a very much higher level, and will have transformed his entire astral body into Manas or Spirit-Self, his entire ether body into Budhi or Life-Spirit and his whole physical body into Atman or Spirit-Man.

Compare this human being as he will appear to us at the end of our earthly course with the same human creature as he appeared at its beginning. In the beginning there was only the physical body, and it was permeated by an ether and an astral body and an ego, but these belonged to divine higher beings who only dwelt within it. At the end of the Earth's evolutionary course, the human being will be entirely permeated by his ego. And this ego itself dwells within the astral body, when as Manas or Spirit-Self it permeates this astral body. The ego then permeates the ether body, which becomes impregnated by Budhi or Life-Spirit and the physical body becomes entirely transfused by Atman or Spirit-Man, also the product of the ego. What a tremendous difference between the creature at the beginning of this evolution and the same human being as he will be at the end of it! But by bringing this great difference clearly before our minds, what I purposely called a contradiction—the sleep state—then becomes comprehensible to us. The very form of the explanation in Esoteric Christianity makes it entirely intelligible to us. What then is this physical body that we shall have before us when the earth has reached the goal of its evolution? Will it be the present physical body? Not in any sense will it be the present physical body, but what the ego shall have made of it. This physical body, as well as the ether and astral bodies, will be wholly spirit-filled. But they were spirit-filled even before the human being transformed them into spirit through the activity of his ego. Even the stone, as we have said, is today permeated by the ether and astral bodies, and ego belonging to it, although they exist in higher spiritual realms.

Thus we see that Esoteric Christianity has good reason for stating that the human being cannot yet master what he today possesses as physical body, because he has not yet reached the end of his evolution when his ego will have worked down even into the physical body. He also cannot yet master the ether body. He will only be able to master that when the Earth has reached the Venus state. Thus he cannot yet master physical and ether bodies through his ego. Only when he has developed Budhi and Atman will he be able to do this. But a physical and ether body of this kind must be controlled in a spiritual way. What the human being himself will some day be able to give to the physical and ether bodies must already be present within them. Those spiritual parts which the ego will at some time give to the ether and physical bodies must be there even now. They were already within the physical body in the beginning when the human creature was in the Saturn Evolution; they were in him when he was on the Sun, and they have continued to remain within him ever since. Thus Esoteric Christianity speaks truly when it says: When the human being has reached the summit of his evolution, what is now already within the human physical body, the divine Atman, a divine spiritual being, will then become a part of it. Budhi also is already within the ether body, but it is the divine Life-Spirit. The human astral body consists, as we have said, of two parts, one of which has been mastered by the human being and another which has not. What, then, is present there within that part which he cannot yet control? It is the Spirit-Self, but a divine Spirit-Self. The real spiritual life of mankind is only present in that part of the astral body in which the ego has already been active since the first incarnation. Thus we have the human being before us.

Let us now look at him in his waking state. What shall we say? The physical body as it appears to us is only the exterior. Within, he is what may be called an atmic being. Interiorly, he is composed of and permeated by higher divine-spiritual beings. The same is true of the ether body. Exteriorly, it is what holds the physical body together; interiorly it is the divine Life-Spirit. And the astral body also is permeated by a divine being, the Spirit-Self. But out of this whole combination, the transformed portion of the astral body alone has been mastered by the ego.

Let us now observe the human being while he sleeps. Here this contradiction disappears at once. We approach him when he is in this state and observe that, as astral body and ego, he is outside the physical body. He calmly abandons it and the ether body every night. Were he to leave the physical body without its being cared for by a divine-spiritual being, he would find it again, but in a shattered condition. A divine-spiritual physical and a divine-spiritual ether are present within the physical and ether bodies and they remain there while these bodies are lying in bed, with the astral body and ego outside. The physical body and ether body are permeated by beings of an atmic and budhic nature.

Now, look back to the beginning of our earthly evolution when nothing in the human being had yet been mastered by the ego. Before his first incarnation the ego was not yet united with the three other members, the physical, ether, and astral bodies. These last came over from the Moon, but the ego did not enter them until the Earth period. On the other hand, a divine Ego was present within them. They would not have been able to exist had not this divine Ego completely permeated them. The astral body was permeated by a divine Spirit-Self, the ether body by a divine Life-Spirit and the physical body by a divine Atman or Spirit-Man.

Let us look back still further to the Moon, Sun, and Saturn evolutions. Upon Saturn, the divine Life-Spirit—which still in the night dwells within the human being lying in bed—had the power to form the human body, as a matter of fact the physical body, into something like a mineral. During the Sun stage, this Life-Spirit transformed the physical body into something of the nature of a plant and on the Moon it was able to form this body into something that experiences pleasure and pain, but which could not yet say "I" to itself. The physical body passed through these lowest stages.

Now, let us proceed to the real Earth incarnation. Here, by experiencing a further transformation, the physical human body became still more perfected than previously. What had it previously been unable to do? What was yet quite foreign to it? What had the divine Spirit kept within itself? What had it not yet entrusted to the human body? It was the power to express in sound the inner life of the soul. On the Moon, this human body, then at the animal stage, was mute. The capacity to permit the soul-life to express itself outwardly in sounds was still with the Divine. It was not yet entrusted to the body's own being. Although there are also animal creatures today able to utter cries, such sounds are, however, something very different from the human vocal sounds. These animals still exist under quite different conditions from the human creature,—they make sounds, it is true, but it is the Divine within them sounding forth. The power to express the inner feelings of the soul in words was only bestowed upon men here upon the Earth. Before this, they were mute; thus this capacity for speech came with life upon the earth.

Let us consider now for a moment as a whole what we have today brought before our souls. The power of speech, namely the Word, was originally with the Divine, and the whole of evolution was so directed that the Godhead first created, as pre-requisite, a physical apparatus which only later acquired the power to allow this Word to sound forth out of itself. Everything was thus guided and directed. Like the flower within its seed, the tone-uttering human being, endowed with the Word or Logos, existed already in germ upon Saturn. Sound was concealed within this germ and developed out of it just as the whole plant grows out of the seed in which it has been hidden.

Let us look back upon the physical human body as it existed upon Saturn and ask ourselves:—Whence came this physical human body? What was its primal source? What did it need to carry it through the whole of evolution?—It came from the Logos or the Word. For even as early as the Saturn period this physical human body was directed in such a way that it later became capable of speech, became a witness of the Logos. That you are formed as you are today, that this human body has its present shape, rests upon the fact that the "Word" lies at the very foundation of the whole plan of our creation. The whole human body has been constructed upon the Word and from the very beginning it was so endowed that at last the Word was able to spring forth from it. When, therefore, the esoteric Christian, looking at this physical human body, asked: What is its original prototype and what is its image? the answer was: This physical human body has its origin in the Word or Logos. This Word or Logos was active from the beginning within the physical human body—

and it is still active there today when the physical body lies in bed deserted by the ego. During that time, the divine Logos is active within the members thus forsaken by the human soul. If we ask: What was the very first beginning of the physical body? then the answer is:—The Logos or the Word.

We shall now follow evolution still further. Saturn passed over into the Sun Period; and then to the human physical body, the life or ether body was added. But what must have entered in order that such a step forward could be made? While on Saturn, the physical body was a kind of machine, a sort of automaton, wholly permeated and maintained, however, by the Logos; on the Sun, the life body was added within which the divine Life-Spirit was active. During the Saturn Period, the human body was an expression of the Logos; then Saturn disappeared, and this human body was reborn upon the Sun. To the physical body was added the life body, permeated by the Life-Spirit. The Logos became Life upon the Sun, while advancing the human creature to a higher stage. The Logos became Life upon the Sun!

Let us now continue further. Upon the Moon, the astral body was added to this human creature. What is the astral body? It appears to the clairvoyant consciousness, even today, like an aura surrounding the human being. It is a body of light, only it cannot be seen in the present state of consciousness. But when seen with clairvoyant vision, it appears as Light, spiritual Light. Our physical light is only transformed spiritual Light and the physical sunlight is the embodiment of the divine-spiritual auric, cosmic Light which is its source. In the present world there is a light streaming down upon us from the sun. But there is yet another light which streams forth out of our own inner radiance. Upon the Moon, the human astral body still shone for the beings in its environment. Thus upon the Moon, the human astral body was united with the physical and ether bodies.

Let us now observe the progress of evolution as a whole. Upon Saturn, we have the physical body as the expression of the Logos; upon the Sun, the ether body is added as an expression of the Life-Spirit. The Logos becomes Life. Upon the Moon, the light-body is added: Life becomes Light! Here we have the story of the evolution of the human body. When the human being began life upon the Earth, he was a creation of the divine-spiritual powers. At that time he existed because within his physical, ether, and astral bodies the Logos was living, the Logos which was Life and which became Light. What now occurred upon the Earth? In the human being and for the human being the ego now entered, and because of this, he was now able not only to live in Light and in Life, but also became capable of observing everything externally, capable of confronting the Logos, Life, and Light. Therefore everything became material to him and he acquired a physical material existence.

Now that we have developed our train of thought thus far, we have approximately reached the point where we shall begin our next lecture, when we shall show how the human creature, born out of the Godhead, has developed into the present ego-being. For we see that prior to this present ego-being, there existed a divine pre-human creature. All that part which has been mastered by the ego is each night torn away from the physical and ether bodies, but the part which from the beginning has always been there within him remains and watches over these bodies when unconcerned, the soul faithlessly deserts them. This original divine-spiritual being remains firmly implanted there.

All that we have been trying to present in the language of Esoteric Christianity, deep mysteries of existence familiar to those who were "servants of the Logos in the earliest times," all this is presented unequivocally in sublime, clear-cut verses in the Gospel of St. John. One must, however, translate these first words in the right way, in conformity with their meaning. Properly translated, these words give the actual facts which have just been presented. Let us bring these facts again before our souls, in order that we may fully comprehend their value.

In the beginning was the Logos which was the archetype of the physical human body, the foundation of all things. All animals, plants and minerals appeared later, for the human creature alone was present upon Saturn. In the Sun Period, the animal kingdom was added, in the Moon Period, the plant kingdom and upon the Earth the mineral kingdom appeared. Upon the Sun, the Logos became Life and upon the Moon, it became Light; then when the human creature became endowed with an ego, the Logos as Light confronted him. But he had to learn to know the nature of the Logos and learn in what form It eventually would make its appearance. First there was the Logos which became Life, then Light, and this Light lives in the astral body. Into the human inner being, into the darkness, into the ignorance, the Light shone. And the meaning of life upon Earth is this:—That men should overcome this darkness of the soul, in order that they may recognize the Light of the Logos.

The first words of the Gospel of St. John are incisive, although, perhaps, very difficult to understand, as many may say. But should the most profound mysteries of the world be expressed in trivial language? Is it not a strange point of view, a real insult to what is Holy when one says, for example, that in order to understand a watch one must penetrate deeply into the nature of the thing with the understanding, but for a comprehension of the Divine in the world, the simple, plain, naive human intelligence should suffice? It is a very bad thing for present humanity that it has reached the point of saying, when reference is made to the profoundness of religious documents: O! why all these complicated explanations? It should all be plain and simple. However, only those who have the good intention and good will to plunge down into the great cosmic facts can penetrate into the deep meaning of such words as those at the very beginning of the most profound of the gospels, this Gospel of St. John, words that are in fact a paraphrase of Spiritual Science.

Let us now translate the introductory words of this Gospel:

In the beginning was the Word and the Word was with God and the Word was a God (or divine). This was in the beginning with God. Through the same all things were made and save through this Word, nothing was made. In It was Life, and Life became the Light of men. And the Light shone into the darkness, but the darkness comprehended it not.

How the darkness, little by little, comes to an understanding of the Light is recounted later on in the Gospels.

III

THE MISSION OF THE EARTH

Yesterday we saw what profound contents are concealed within the first words of the Gospel of St. John and we shall now be able to summarize our observations by saying that the writer of this Gospel pointed to the creation of a pre-humanity in the far distant past and indicated that, according to Esoteric Christianity, everything leads back to the Word or the Logos. The Logos was already a creating power even in the ancient Saturn Period; it then became Life while our Earth was passing through its existence as the Sun, and it became Light while the Earth was passing through the ancient Moon state. Under the influence of divine spiritual forces and powers, in the course of the three planetary states of evolution, the human creature reached the point in his development at which he became penetrated by the human ego, the Earth having now developed into our present planet. Thus we may say that a creature, like a kind of seed, came over to the Earth from the ancient Moon, consisting of a physical body, derived from the divine, primal Word; an ether or life body having its source in divine Life; and an astral body issuing from divine Light. Within this creature's inmost being, during life upon the Earth, the light of the ego itself was now enkindled and this three-fold bodily nature, physical, etheric and astral, became capable of saying to itself "I AM." Thus, in a certain sense, we may call the Earth evolution, the evolution of the "I AM," the evolution of the self-consciousness of the human race. This "I AM," this capacity for full self-consciousness, developed slowly and gradually in the course of the evolution of Earth humanity. We must clearly understand how this evolution of Earth humanity proceeded, how slowly and gradually the ego, that is to say, full self-consciousness, made its appearance within it.

There was a stage of our earthly evolution which we call the ancient Lemurian period. It is the earliest period of our life upon the Earth in which men appeared in the form they, in general, possess today. Then, for the first time, what we may call the incarnation of the ego, the true inner being of man, took place within the three bodies, the astral, ether and physical bodies. After that came the Atlantean period when humanity dwelt for the most part upon the ancient continent of Atlantis, a region forming today the bed of the Atlantic Ocean, and which sank beneath the waters through the great Atlantean flood, remembrance of which has been preserved in the deluge-sagas of nearly all peoples. In harmony with their inner natures, men have passed through successive incarnations during the post-Atlantean period right up to our present day. As has been stated, it was in fact during the Lemurian period that our souls were incarnated for the first time in a three-fold entity, consisting of physical body, ether body and astral body, as we have learned to know them. What preceded this will be left for a later consideration. Thus we must go far back into the past if we wish to consider the course of evolution, for the human being evolved very slowly and gradually to his present condition of existence.

From the standpoint of Spiritual Science what does occultism call our "present existence?" It calls it a state of consciousness which the present day human being possesses from the morning when he awakens until the evening when he falls asleep. During that time, by means of his outer physical senses, he sees the objects about him. From the evening when he falls asleep, until the morning when he awakens, he does not see the objects about him. Why is this so? We know that it is because during the day, under present evolutionary conditions, the real inner human being, namely, the ego and astral body, are within the physical and ether bodies upon the physical plane; in other words, they are in the physical world. Thus the astral body and the ego can make use of the physical organs for hearing and seeing in the physical world, for observing physical things. From the evening when we fall asleep, until the morning when we awaken, the ego and astral body are out of the physical world on the astral plane. There they are detached from the physical eyes and ears and therefore are not able to observe what is about them.

The alternating state of waking by day and sleeping by night developed slowly and gradually. This was not yet the case in the ancient Lemurian period when the human being for the first time passed through a physical incarnation. At that time the ego and astral body were only for a very brief portion of the day within the physical body, by no means as long a period as now. Therefore, because the human being was outside of his physical body for a longer time and entered it only for a brief period in a waking state, life during the Lemurian period was very different from life as we experience it. Our state of unconsciousness during the night, when we are not merely in the act of dreaming, is a state that has developed slowly and gradually. Day and night consciousness were very differently apportioned during the Lemurian period. At that time everyone still possessed a dull clairvoyant consciousness, and during the night, when they were out of the physical body and in the spirit world, they perceived this spirit world around them, although not so clearly as we of the present see the physical objects about us during the day. We should not simply compare this perceiving in the spiritual world with the present dreaming. The present dream-state is only like a last stunted remnant of this ancient clairvoyance. However, the same images were perceived at that time as are perceived today in dreams, but they had a very real meaning. Let us be quite clear about the meaning of these images.

In ancient times, the human being, living a very brief portion of the twenty-four hours in waking-consciousness (a much shorter time than we today), saw the external, physical objects very dimly as though wrapped in a mist. The capacity to see physical objects as we do today developed very slowly. At that time he saw the first indication of a physical body enveloped in a mist just as we can see the lamps surrounded by a mist, by a kind of light-aura, when we walk through the streets on a misty evening. This, however, is only an illusion. But that is the way mankind at first saw physical bodies emerging about him, and when he slept he did not sink into unconsciousness, but during his sleep-consciousness, images emerged, pictures in colour and form. At that time there was around him a world, in comparison with which, the most vivid dream-world of today is only a weak, dim echo. These images signified something psychic and spiritual in his environment. At that time, in the beginning of his earthly course, when during his night wanderings he approached a creature harmful to him, he did not see it as we would now see it—for example, he did not see the lion approaching him as a lion's form—but he saw emerging an image of colour and form and instinctively it told him that here was something harmful to him, something that would devour him, something he must avoid. These were true images of something psycho-spiritual occurring about him. All that belonged to the soul and spirit was seen in the night, and evolution proceeded in such a way that slowly and gradually the human being immersed himself in his physical body for a longer and longer time. Ever shorter grew the night, longer and longer lasted the day, and the more he lived within his physical body, the more the nightly clairvoyant images disappeared and the more did the present waking-consciousness emerge.

However, we must not forget that a truly genuine self-consciousness, such as should be acquired during life upon the earth, can only be attained by submersion in a physical body. Prior to this, the human being did not feel himself as an independent entity, but as a part of divine spiritual beings from whom he was descended. Still possessing a dull clairvoyance, he felt himself a part of a divine spiritual consciousness, part of a divine ego, just as the hand feels itself a part of the physical organism. He could not have said of himself "I AM," but would have said "God is"—and "I in Him."

As we shall see more and more, a very special mission was reserved for the Earth, which had, during its evolution, passed through three earlier stages, Saturn, Sun and Moon. Do not imagine that the different planetary life-conditions can be considered as existing alongside of one another, one planet exactly equivalent to the other. Divine creation is not simply a repetition of something already existing. Each planetary existence had a very definite mission. The mission of our Earth is the cultivation of the principle of love to its highest degree by those beings who are evolving upon it. When the Earth has reached the end of its evolution, love should permeate it through and through. Let us understand clearly what is meant by the expression: The Earth is the planetary life-condition for the evolution of love.

In Spiritual Science we say that the ancient Moon preceded the Earth. This ancient Moon, as planetary stage of evolution, had also a mission. It did not yet have the task of developing love, but it was the planet or the cosmos of wisdom. Before it reached our earthly condition, our planet passed through the stage of wisdom. A simple and one might say logical observation will illustrate this to you. Just look about you at all the creatures of nature. If you do not observe them merely with your understanding but with the forces of your heart and soul, then you will find wisdom everywhere stamped upon nature. The wisdom of which we are here speaking, is a kind of spiritual substance lying at the foundation of all things. Observe anything you wish in nature, and you will find it there. Take, for example, a piece of the thigh-bone and you will see that it is not composed of a solid mass, but it is a fine interweaving of supports which are arranged into a marvelous structure. And if we seek to discover the law upon which this bone is constructed, we find that it follows the law which develops the greatest strength with the least expenditure of material in order to be able to support the upper part of the human body. Our engineering art is not yet so far advanced that it can build such a highly artistic structure as the all over-ruling wisdom has fashioned. Mankind will not possess such wisdom until later in its evolution. *Divine* wisdom pervades the whole of nature; *human* wisdom will only gradually reach this height. In the course of time human wisdom will inwardly acquire what divine wisdom has secreted within the Earth. Just as wisdom was prepared upon the Moon, that it might be found everywhere on the Earth, so is love now being prepared here in this Earth evolution. If you were able to look back upon the ancient Moon with clairvoyant vision, you would see that wisdom was not to be found everywhere at that time. You would find many things still lacking in wisdom. Only gradually throughout the whole of the Moon evolution was wisdom stamped upon the outer world. When the Moon had fully completed its evolution, everything was then pervaded by a wisdom which was to be found everywhere. *Inner* wisdom first appeared upon the Earth with the human being, with the ego. This inner human wisdom had to be developed by degrees.

Just as wisdom was evolved upon the Moon, in order that it might now be found in all things, so in like manner is love evolving. Love came into existence first in its lowest, its most sensuous form, during the Lemurian period, but during the course of life upon the earth, it will become ever more and more spiritualized, until at last, when the earth has reached the end of its evolution, the whole of existence will have become pervaded with love, as today it is pervaded with wisdom, and this will be accomplished through the activity of human beings if they but fulfil their task.

The Earth will then pass over to a future planetary condition which is called Jupiter. The beings who will wander about upon Jupiter, just as human beings move about upon the earth, will find love exhaling from all creatures, the love which they themselves, as human beings, will have placed there during their life upon the earth. They will find love in everything just as we today find wisdom everywhere. Then human beings will develop love out of their own inner selves in the same way that they are now little by little evolving wisdom. The great cosmic love that here upon the Earth is beginning its existence will then permeate all things. The materialistic mind does not believe in a cosmic wisdom, only in a human wisdom. If men would consider the course of evolution with unprejudiced minds, they would be able to see that all cosmic wisdom in the beginning of the Earth's evolution was advanced as far as human wisdom will be at the end of it. In those times when names were more accurately chosen than they are today, the subjective wisdom active in the human being was called "intelligence," in contra-distinction to the objective cosmic wisdom. Men do not notice that what they discover in the course of Earth-life had already been won during life upon the Moon and implanted in the earth by divine-spiritual beings. Let us take an example.

How it is drummed into the heads of the school children, the great progress humanity has made through the discovery of paper! But wasps had already produced paper many thousands of years ago, for what the wasps build into their nests consists of exactly the same substance as that out of which men now produce paper and it is produced by the wasp in exactly the same way—only by means of a life-process. The wasp-spirit, the group-soul of the wasps, which is a part of divine-spiritual substance, was the discoverer of paper long before men made the discovery.

The human being, in fact, always follows along groping his way behind the cosmic wisdom. As a principle, all that men will discover in the course of the Earth's evolution is already present in nature. But what the human being will really give to the Earth is love, a love which will evolve from the most sensuous to the most spiritualized form of love. This is the mission of the Earth-evolution. The Earth is the cosmos of love.

Let us ask:—What then is essential for love? What is essential in order that one person love another? It is this—that he be in possession of his full self-consciousness, that he be wholly independent. No one can love another in the full sense of the word if this love be not a free gift of one person to another. My hand does not love my organism. Only one who is independent, one who is not bound to the other person, can love him.

To this end the human being had to become an ego-being. The ego had to be implanted in the threefold human body, so that the Earth might, through mankind, fulfil its mission of love. Therefore, you will understand Esoteric Christianity when it says:—Just as other forces, of which wisdom is the last, streamed down from divine beings during the Moon period, so now love streams into the Earth and the bearer of love can only be the independent ego which develops by degrees in the course of the evolution of the Earth.

The human being, however, had to be very slowly prepared for all this, likewise for his present kind of consciousness. Let us suppose, for instance, that in the ancient Lemurian period, the human being had been immersed in his physical body—he would then at that time have seen the full outer reality, but at such a swift tempo he would not have been able to implant love in the world. He had to be guided little by little to his earthly mission. The first instruction in love was given him during the time of a dawning consciousness, before he possessed full self-consciousness, before he was evolved far enough to observe the objects about him with clear, waking-day consciousness. Thus we see that during those ages when the human being still possessed an ancient, dreamy clairvoyant consciousness, when the soul was for long periods outside the physical body, love was being implanted within him in his dull, not yet self-conscious condition. Let us clearly picture the soul of this human creature of olden times which had not yet reached the height of full self-consciousness.

The human being fell asleep at night, but there existed no abrupt transition from waking to sleeping. Images emerged, vivid dream-pictures, which, however, possessed a living relationship to the spirit world—this means that the human creature familiarized himself with the spirit world during sleep. Into him, into his dull state of consciousness, the Divine Spirit dropped the first seed of all love activity. The power that manifests itself as love in the course of evolution on the Earth streamed at first into mankind during the night. The God who brought the true earthly mission to the Earth revealed Himself first in the night to the dim, ancient clairvoyant consciousness before He could reveal Himself to clear, waking day-consciousness.

Then slowly and gradually the time spent in a dim, clairvoyant state of consciousness became shorter and shorter, the day-consciousness became ever longer, and the boundaries of the aura around the physical objects gradually lessened and disappeared, the objects taking on clearer and clearer outlines. Formerly the sun and moon were seen surrounded by a mighty halo as though lying in a mass of fog. Only slowly did the whole aspect become clear and objects assume distinct outlines. By degrees the human being arrived at this condition. What he then saw externally, while the sun shone upon the earth, revealing to him by means of visible light the whole of earth-life, minerals, plants and animals—all this he experienced as the revelations of the Divine in the outer world.

From the standpoint of Esoteric Christianity, what is it that is visible during waking-day consciousness? In the broadest sense of the word, we may ask:—Of what does the Earth consist? It is a manifestation of divine powers, an outer material manifestation of inner spirituality. If you turn your gaze upward toward the sun or toward what is to be found upon the earth, you will see everywhere a manifestation of Divine-Spirituality. This Divine-Spirituality, in the present form, lying as it does at the foundation of all that appears to clear, waking-day consciousness, in other words, the invisible world behind this entire visible day-world, this is called in Esoteric Christianity, the "Logos" or the "Word." For just as from the human being speech can finally come forth, be uttered from his own inner being, so too has everything, animal kingdom, plant kingdom, mineral kingdom first come forth into existence from the Logos. Everything is an incarnation of the Logos and just as your soul rules invisibly within your inner being and creates an external body, so too everything in the world of a soul nature creates for itself the external body fitted to it and manifests itself through some sort of physical organism. Where, then, is the physical body of the Logos, of which the Gospel of St. John speaks? It is this we wish today to bring more and more into our consciousness. In its purest form, this external physical body of the Logos appears especially in the outer sunlight. But the sunlight is not merely material light. To spiritual perception, it is just as much the vesture of the Logos, as your outer physical body is the vesture of your soul.

If you were to confront a human being in the same way the greater part of humanity today confronts the sun, you could never learn to know that human being. Your relation to each human individual possessing a feeling, thinking and willing soul would be such that instead of presupposing a psycho-spiritual part within him, you would simply touch a physical body and imagine that it might even be made of *papier maché*. If, however, you wish to penetrate to the spiritual in the sunlight, you should consider it just as you consider the bodily part of a human being in order to learn to know his inner nature. The sunlight has the same relationship to the Logos as your body has to your soul. In the sunlight something spiritual streams down upon the Earth. If we are able to conceive not only the sun-body, but also the sun-spirit, we find that this spiritual part is the love that streams down upon the Earth. Not alone the physical sunlight awakens the plants into life—they would wither and die if the physical sunlight did not act upon them—but together with the physical sunlight, the warm love of the Godhead streams to earth. Human beings exist in order that they may take into themselves the warm love of the Divine, develop it and return it again to the Divine. But they can only do this by becoming self-conscious ego-beings. Only then will they be able to render back this love.

When men began—at first for a very short time—to live in waking-day consciousness, they could perceive nothing of the light, that light which at the same time enkindled love. The light shone into the darkness, but the darkness was unable yet to comprehend it. If this light, which is at the same time the love of the Logos, had only manifested itself during the short day hours, humanity would not have been able to grasp this light of love. But love streamed into human beings in the dull clairvoyant dream-consciousness of those ancient times. Now, let us glance behind existence at a great significant cosmic mystery.

Let us express it thus:—The cosmic guidance of our earth was of such a character that for a time, in an unconscious way, love streamed into humanity in its dim, clairvoyant state of consciousness and inwardly prepared it to receive this love in full, clear, waking-day consciousness. We have seen that our Earth gradually became the cosmos that was to accomplish this mission of love. The earth is shone upon by the present sun. Just as human beings dwell upon the earth, and little by little receive love into themselves, so too do other much higher beings dwell upon the sun and enkindle love, because the sun has reached a higher stage of existence. The human being is an earth-dweller and to be an earth-dweller means to be a creature which appropriates love unto itself during the Earth-period. A sun-dweller in our time means a being that can enkindle love, a being that can permit love to flow into the earth. The earth-dweller would not have developed love, would not have been able to receive it, had not the sun-dwellers sent down ripened wisdom to them with the rays of light. Because the light of the sun streams down upon the earth, love is developed there. That is a very real truth. Those beings who are so exalted that they can pour forth love have made the sun their scene of action.

When the ancient Moon had completed its evolution, there were seven great beings of this kind who had progressed far enough to pour forth love. Here we touch upon a deep mystery which Spiritual Science reveals. In the beginning of the Earth-evolution, there was on the one side the childlike humanity which was to receive love and become ready for the reception of the ego—and on the other side there was the sun which separated from the earth and rose to a more exalted existence. Seven principle Spirits of Light, who at the same time were the dispensing Spirits of Love, were able to evolve upon this sun. Only six of them, however, made the sun their dwelling-place and what streams down to us in the physical light of the sun contains within it the spiritual force of love from these six Spirits of Light or, as they are called in the Bible, the six Elohim. One separated from the others and took a different path for the salvation of humanity. He did not choose the sun but the moon for his abode. And this Spirit of Light, who voluntarily renounced life upon the sun and chose the moon instead, is none other than the one whom the Old Testament calls "Jahve" or "Jehova". This Spirit of Light who chose the moon as a dwelling-place is the one who from there pours ripened wisdom down upon the earth, thus preparing the way for love. Now, let us consider for a moment this mystery which lies behind the outer facts.

The night belongs to the moon and it belonged to the moon to a much greater degree in that ancient time when the human being was not yet able to receive the force of love in the direct rays of the sun. At that time he received the reflected force of ripened wisdom from the moonlight. This ripened wisdom streamed down upon him from the moonlight during the time of night-consciousness. Therefore, Jahve is called the Ruler of the Night who prepared humanity for the love that was later to manifest during full waking-consciousness. Thus we can look back to that ancient past in human evolution when spiritually that event occurred which is merely symbolized by the heavenly bodies, the sun on the one side, the moon on the other. (See drawing). During the night, at certain times, the moon sends down to us the reflected force of the sun, but it is the same light which also shines upon us directly from the sun. Thus in ancient times, Jahve or Jehova reflected the force of matured wisdom, the force of the six Elohim, and sent this force down into human beings while they slept, preparing them to become capable later, by degrees, of receiving the power of love during waking-day consciousness.

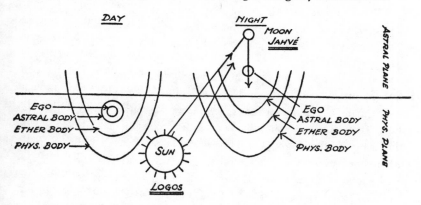

The above drawing attempts in a symbolic manner to show the waking-day human being when his physical and etheric bodies are dependent upon the Divine and his ego and astral body are within the physical and ether bodies upon the physical plane. Here the whole human organism is shone upon by the sun from without. We now know that for the humanity of primeval ages, night was much longer and much more filled with activity than it is at present. The astral body and ego were then outside of the physical and ether bodies, the ego existing wholly within the astral world, and the astral body sinking into the physical body from without, having, however, its entire inner being still embedded in the divine-spiritual world. Therefore, the sun could not shine directly upon the human astral body and enkindle in it the force of love. Hence, the moon, which reflects the sunlight, was active through Jahve or Jehova.

The moon is the symbol of Jahve or Jehova and the sun is none other than the symbol for the Logos, which is the sum of the other six Elohim. This drawing, which you should study, and upon which you should meditate, tries to indicate this in a symbolic way and if you reflect upon it, you will discern what deep, mystery-truths are presented in it, namely: that during long periods of time, in sleep-consciousness, the force of love was being implanted in human beings by Jehova, in a manner of which they were themselves unconscious. In this way they were being made capable of experiencing the Logos, of feeling the force of Its love. One can ask:—How was this possible, how could that take place? We come now to the other side of the mystery.

We have said that the human being was destined for self-conscious love upon the earth. He must, therefore, have a leader, a teacher, during his clear day-consciousness, a leader who stands before him so that he can be perceived by him. Now it was only during the night, in dim consciousness, that love could be implanted within the human being. But little by little something happened, something happened in full actuality which made it possible for him to see outwardly, physically, the Being of Love itself. But how could that occur? It could only take place, because the Being of Divine Love, the Being of the Logos, became a man of flesh, whom men by means of their physical senses could perceive upon the earth. It was because mankind had developed to a condition of perceiving by means of outer senses that God, the Logos, had Himself to become a sense-being. He had to appear in a physical body. This was fulfilled in Christ-Jesus, and the historical appearance of Christ Jesus means that the forces of the six Elohim, or of the Logos, were incarnated in Jesus of Nazareth at the beginning of our Christian era and were actually present in Him in the visible world. That is the important thing. The inner force of the sun, the force of the Logos-Love assumed a physical human form in the body of Jesus of Nazareth. For, like an external object, like an outer being, God had to appear to the earthly, human sense-consciousness in a bodily form.

You will ask what was that Being Who appears at the beginning of our era as Christ-Jesus? It was the incarnation of the Logos, of the six other Elohim, whose advent had been prepared by Jahve-God who preceded them. This figure of Jesus of Nazareth, in whom the Christ or the Logos was incarnated, brought into human life, into human history itself, what previously streamed down upon the earth from the sun, what was present only in the sunlight. "The Logos became flesh." It is upon this fact that the Gospel of St. John places the greatest importance and the writer of this Gospel had to lay great emphasis upon it because it is a fact that after the appearance of a few initiated Christian pupils who understood what had occurred, there followed others who could not fully understand it. They understood full well that at the foundation of all material things, behind all that appears to us in substantial form, there exists a psycho-spiritual world. But what they could not comprehend was that the Logos itself, by being incarnated in an individual human being, became physically visible for the physical sense-world. This they could not comprehend. Therefore, that teaching which appeared in the early Christian centuries called the "Gnosis," differs from the true Esoteric Christianity on this point. The writer of the Gospel of St. John pointed to this fact in powerful words, when he said: "No, you should not look upon the Christ as a supersensible, ever invisible being only, one Who is the foundation of all material life, but you should consider this the important thing: 'The Word became flesh and dwelt among us'." This is the fine distinction between Esoteric Christianity and the primal Gnosis. The Gnosis, as well as Esoteric Christianity recognizes the Christ, but the former only as a spiritual being and in Jesus of Nazareth it sees at most a human herald, more or less bound to this spiritual being. It holds firmly to an ever invisible Christ. On the contrary, Esoteric Christianity has always held the idea of the Gospel of St. John, which rests upon the firm foundation of the words: "And the Logos became flesh and dwelt among us!" He Who was there in the visible world is an actual incarnation of the six sun Elohim, of the Logos! With the incarnation of the Logos, the earthly mission—or in other words, what the earth was to become through the Event of Palestine—first really began. Previously, all was only a preparation.

What then did the Christ, who dwelt within the body of Jesus of Nazareth, especially have to represent Himself to be? It may be said He had to represent himself as the great bringer and quickener of the self-conscious, independent human being. Let us express this living Christ-teaching in a few short, paradigmatic sentences. The earth exists in order that full self-consciousness, the "I AM," may be given to mankind. Previously, everything was a preparation for this self-consciousness, for this "I AM;" and the Christ was that Being Who gave the impulse that made it possible for every human being—each as an individual—to experience the "I AM." Only with His advent was the powerful impulse given which carries earth humanity forward with a mighty bound. We can follow this by means of a comparison of Christianity with the Old Testament teaching. In the latter, the human being did not yet fully feel the "I AM" in himself. He still possessed a remnant of a dreamy state of consciousness, held over from those ancient times when he did not feel himself as a personality, but as a part of a Divine Being, just as the animal today is still a member of a group-soul. Mankind had its beginning in the group-soul and then advanced to a state of independent, personal existence, in which every individual experiences the "I AM," and the Christ is the force that has brought it to this consciousness of the "I AM." Let us consider this for a moment in its full inner significance.

The follower of the Old Testament did not feel himself as much enclosed within his own individual personality as did the follower of the New Testament. He did not yet say as a personality, "I am an I." He felt himself within the whole ancient Jewish people and experienced the group-ego of his folk. Let us enter in a living way into the consciousness of a follower of the Old Testament. The Christian feels the "I AM" and gradually will learn to feel it more and more, but the follower of the Old Testament did not feel the "I AM" in this way. He felt himself as a member of the entire folk and looked up to its group-soul. And if he wished to express this in words, he would have said: "My consciousness reaches up to the Father of the whole people, to Abraham; we—I and Father Abraham—are one. A common ego encompasses us all, and I only feel myself safe within the spiritual substantiality of the world when I feel myself resting within the whole folk-substance." Thus the follower of the Old Testament looked up to Father Abraham and said: "I and Father Abraham are one! In my veins flows the same blood that flows in the veins of Abraham." He felt Father Abraham as the root from which every individual Abrahamite had sprung as a stem.

Then Christ-Jesus came and said to his nearest, most intimate initiates: Hitherto, mankind has judged only according to the flesh, according to blood-relationship. Through this blood-relationship, men have been conscious of reposing within a higher invisible union. But you should believe in a still higher spiritual relationship, in one that reaches beyond the blood-tie. You should believe in a spiritual Father-substance in which the ego is rooted, and which is more spiritual than the substance which as a group-soul binds the Jewish people together. You should believe in what reposes within me and within every human being, in what is not only one with Abraham, but one with the very divine foundation of the world. Therefore Christ-Jesus, according to the Gospel of St. John, emphasizes the words: "Before Father Abraham was, was the I AM!" My primal ego mounts not only to the Father-Principle that reaches back to Abraham, but my ego is one with all that pulses through the entire cosmos, and to this my spiritual nature soars aloft. I and the Father are one! These are important words which one should experience; then will one feel the forward bound made by mankind, a bound which advanced human evolution further in consequence of that impulse given by the advent of the Christ. The Christ was the mighty quickener of the "I AM."

Now, let us try to hear a little of what His most intimate initiates said, how they expressed what had been revealed to them. They said: Heretofore, no individual physical human being has ever existed to whom this name of "I AM" could be applied; He was the first to bring to the world the "I AM" in its full significance. Therefore, they named Christ-Jesus the "I AM." That was the name in which the closest initiates felt themselves united, the name which they understood, the name "I AM." We must in this way delve deeply into the most significant chapters of the Gospel of St. John. If we take that chapter where we find the words: "I am the Light of the world," we must interpret them literally, quite literally. Now, what was this "I AM" which for the first time appeared in carnate form? It was the force of the Logos that streamed to earth in the sunlight. All through the entire eighth chapter, beginning with the twelfth verse which is usually entitled "Jesus, the Light of the World," we find a transcription of this profound truth concerning the meaning of the "I AM." When you read this chapter, emphasize the words "I" or "I AM" wherever they appear and realize that "I AM" was the *name* in

which the initiates felt themselves united. Then you will understand it
and it will seem to you that this chapter must then be read in somewhat
the following manner:

Then Jesus spoke to His disciples and said: That which is able
to say "I AM" to itself, is the Force of the Light of the World, and
whoever follows after me will see in clear, waking consciousness
what those who wander in darkness do not see.

But those who clung to the old belief that only by night can the
Light of Love be implanted within the human being, those who were
called the Pharisees, answered: Thou callest upon thy "I AM" but
we call upon Father Abraham. In this way we feel the power which
justifies us in acting as self-conscious beings. We feel ourselves
strong when we immerse ourselves in the substance of a common ego
which reaches to—Father Abraham.

Jesus said:—If one speaks of the I, as I speak, then is the testimony a true one; for I know that this I comes from the Father,
from the primeval foundation of the world and I know whither it
tends.

Now, let us consider those important words of Chapter VIII, verse
15, which should be translated in the following manner:—

Ye judge all things according to the flesh, but I judge not the
perishable that is in the flesh.

And if I judge, then is my judgment true. For the I does not exist
for itself alone, but it is united with the Father from whom it has
descended.

That is the meaning of this passage. Thus everywhere you find reference to a common Father. We are now able to bring the idea of the
Father still more clearly before our souls. Then we see that the words,
"Before Father Abraham was, was the I AM," contain the living essence
of the Christian doctrine.

Today we have gone deeply into the words of the Gospel of St. John,
more deeply than we would have been able had I interpreted them from
an external point of view. We have drawn these words out of Spiritual
Wisdom and have alluded to certain important words in the Gospel of St.

John which show the very essentials of Christianity. We shall see that just by understanding such germinal and primal key-words, light and clarity will be brought into the whole of the Gospel.

Let us consider all this as a teaching that was given in the Christian esoteric schools, a teaching which the writer of the Gospel has transcribed —in a way which we shall discuss—in order that he might hand it down to posterity for those who really wish to penetrate into its meaning.

IV

THE RAISING OF LAZARUS

From the three foregoing lectures, it should have become somewhat clear that in the Gospel of St. John the truths of Spiritual Science can be found again. However, it must be very clear that in order to discover these truths, it will be necessary to weigh every word thoroughly. In fact the important thing in a consideration of this religious document is that the true, exact meaning be perfectly understood, for as we shall see in particular instances everything in it has the deepest possible significance. Moreover, not only the wording of special passages is of importance, but something else must be considered and this is the division, the composition, the structure of the document. As a matter of fact, people no longer have the right feeling for such things. Authors of the past—if I may so designate them—introduced into their works much more of an architectural structure, much more of an inner arrangement than is usually imagined. You need only to recall from among them a relatively modern poet, Dante, to find this confirmed. Here we see that the Divine Comedy is architecturally composed of parts based upon the number three. And it is not without meaning that each division of Dante's Comedia closes with the word "Stars." This I mention only to suggest how architecturally ancient writers constructed their works, and especially in the great religious documents we should never lose sight of this architectural form, because in certain cases the form signifies a very great deal. To be sure, we must first discover this meaning.

Here at the end of the 10th Chapter of this Gospel of St. John we should recall the following verse, which we should keep clearly in mind. In the 41st verse we read:—

And many came to him and said:—
John performed no miracles, but all that he said of this man is true.

This means that we find in this verse of the 10th Chapter, an indication that the testimony given of Christ Jesus by John is true. He expresses the truth of this testimony in very special language. Then we come to the end of the Gospel and there we find a corresponding verse. Here we read in the 24th verse of the 21st Chapter:—

This is the disciple which testifieth of these things, and wrote these things: and we know that his testimony is true!

Here at the end of the entire Gospel, we have a statement that the testimony of the one who reported these things is a true one. The coincidence that something very special is being said, here and there, by means of some particular word, is never without significance in ancient writings and just behind this coincidence is concealed something very important. We shall proceed with our considerations in the right manner if we direct our attention to the reason for this.

In the middle of the Gospel of St. John a fact is presented which, if not understood, would render this Gospel incomprehensible. Directly following the passage in which these words are introduced as confirmation of the truth of the testimony of John the Baptist stands the chapter concerning the raising of Lazarus. With this chapter the whole Gospel falls into two parts. At the end of the first part it is pointed out that the testimony of John the Baptist should be accepted for everything that is maintained and affirmed concerning Christ Jesus and at the very end of the Gospel it is pointed out that all that follows the chapter on the raising of Lazarus should be accepted on the testimony of the Disciple whom we have often heard designated as "the Disciple whom the Lord loved." What then is the real meaning of the "raising of Lazarus?"

Let me remind you that following the narration of the raising of Lazarus there stands an apparently enigmatical passage. Let us picture the whole situation:—Christ Jesus performs what is usually called a miracle—in the Gospel itself it is called a "sign"—namely, the raising of Lazarus. And subsequently we find many passages which attest that "this man performs many signs," and all that follows indicates that the accusers did not wish to have intercourse with Him because of these signs. If you read these words, whatever their translation (this has already been referred to in my book *Christianity as Mystical Fact*), you would need to ask:—What is really at the bottom of it all? The raising of some one provoked the enemies of Christ Jesus to rise up against Him. Why should just the raising of Lazarus so provoke these opponents? Why does the persecution of Christ Jesus begin just at this stage? One who knows how to read this Gospel will understand that a mystery lies hidden within this chapter. The mystery concealed therein is, in truth, concerned with the actual identity of the man who says all that we find written there. In order to understand this, we must turn our attention to what in the ancient Mysteries is called "initiation." How did these initiations in the ancient Mysteries take place?

A man who was initiated could himself have experiences and personal knowledge of the spiritual worlds and thus he could bear witness of them. Those who were found sufficiently developed for initiation were led into the Mysteries. Everywhere—in Greece, among the Chaldeans, among the Egyptians and the Indians—these Mysteries existed. There the neophytes were instructed for a long time in approximately the same things which we now learn in Spiritual Science. Then when they were sufficiently instructed, there followed that part of the training which opened up to them the way to a perception of the spiritual world. However, in ancient times this could only be brought about by putting the neophyte into a very extraordinary condition in respect of his four principles—his physical, ether and astral bodies and his ego. The next thing that occurred to the neophyte was that he was put into a death-like sleep by the initiator or hierophant who understood the matter and there he remained for three and a half days. Why this occurred can be seen if we consider that in the present cycle of evolution, when the human being sleeps in the ordinary sense of the word, his physical and ether bodies lie in bed and his astral body and ego are withdrawn. In that condition he cannot observe any of the spiritual events taking place about him, because his astral body has not yet developed the spiritual sense-organs for a perception of the world in which he then finds himself. Only when his astral body and ego have slipped back into his physical and ether bodies, and he once more makes use of his eyes and ears, does he again perceive the physical world, that is, he perceives a world about him. Through what he had learned, the neophyte was capable of developing spiritual organs of perception in his astral body and when he was sufficiently evolved for the astral body to have formed these organs, then all that the astral body had received into itself had to be impressed upon the ether body just as the design on a seal is impressed upon the sealing-wax. This is the important thing. All preparations for initiation depended upon the surrender of the man himself to the inner processes which reorganized his astral body.

The human being at one time did not have eyes and ears in his physical body as he has today, but undeveloped organs instead—just as animals who have never been exposed to the light have no eyes. The light forms the eye, sound fashions the ear. What the neophyte practiced through meditation and concentration and what he experienced inwardly through them, acted like light upon the eye and sound upon the ear. In this way the astral body was transformed and organs of perception for seeing in the astral or higher world were evolved. But these organs are not yet firmly enough fixed in the ether body. They will become so when what has been formed in the astral body will have been stamped upon the ether body. However, as long as the ether body remains bound to the physical, it is not possible for all that has been accomplished by means of spiritual exercises to be really impressed upon it. Before this can happen, the ether body must be drawn out of the physical. Therefore when the ether body was drawn out of the physical body during the three and a half days death-like sleep, all that had been prepared in the astral body was stamped upon the ether body. The neophyte then experienced the spiritual world. Then when he was called back into the physical body by the Priest-Initiator, he bore witness through his own experience of what takes place in the spiritual worlds. This procedure has now become unnecessary through the appearance of Christ-Jesus. This three and a half day death-like sleep can now be replaced by the force proceeding from the Christ. For we shall soon see that in the Gospel of St. John strong forces are present which render it possible for the present astral body, even though the ether body is still within the physical, to have the power to stamp upon the etheric what had previously been prepared within it. But for this to take place, Christ-Jesus must first be present. Up to this time without the above characterized procedure, humanity was not far enough advanced for the astral body to be able to imprint upon the ether body what had been prepared within it through meditation and concentration. This was a process which often took place within the Mysteries; a neophyte was brought into a death-like sleep by the Priest-Initiator and was guided through the higher worlds. He was then again called back into his physical body by the Priest-Initiator and thus became a witness of the spiritual world through his own experience.

This took place always in the greatest secrecy and the outer world knew nothing of the occurrences within these ancient Mysteries. Through Christ-Jesus a new initiation had to arise to replace the old, an initiation produced by means of forces of which we have yet to speak. The old form of initiation must end, but a transition had to be made from the old to the new age and to make this transition, someone had once more to be initiated in the old way, but initiated into Christian Esotericism. This only Christ-Jesus Himself could perform and the neophyte was the one who is called Lazarus. "This sickness is not unto death," means here that it is the three and a half day death-like sleep. This is clearly indicated.

You will see that the presentation is of a very veiled character, but for one who is able to decipher a presentation of this kind it represents initiation. The individuality Lazarus had to be initiated in such a way that he could be a witness of the spiritual worlds. An expression is used, a very significant expression in the language of the Mysteries, "that the Lord loved Lazarus." What does "to love" mean in the language of the Mysteries? It expresses the relationship of the pupil to the teacher. "He whom the Lord loved" is the most intimate, the most deeply initiated pupil. The Lord Himself had initiated Lazarus and as an initiate Lazarus arose from the grave, which means from his place of initiation. This same expression "Whom the Lord loved" is always used later in connection with John, or perhaps we should say in connection with the writer of the Gospel of St. John, for the name "John" is not used. He is the "Beloved Disciple" to whom the Gospel refers. He is the risen Lazarus himself and the writer of the Gospel wished to say:—"What I have to offer, I say by virtue of the initiation which has been conferred upon me by the Lord Himself." Therefore the writer of the Gospel distinguishes between what occurred *before* and what occurred *after* the raising of Lazarus. Before the raising, an initiate of the old order is quoted, one who has attained a knowledge of the Spirit, one whose testimony is repeatedly announced to be true. "However, what is to be said concerning the most profound of matters, concerning the Mystery of Golgotha, I myself say, I the Risen One; but only after I have been raised, can I speak concerning it!" And so we have in the first part of the Gospel, the testimony of the *old* John—in the second half, the testimony of the *new* John whom the Lord Himself had initiated, for this is the risen Lazarus. Only thus do we grasp the real meaning of this chapter. These words are written there because John wished to say:—I call upon the testimony of my supersensible organs, my spiritual powers of perception. What I have related I have not seen in the ordinary physical world, but in the spiritual world in which I have dwelt by virtue of the initiation which the Lord has conferred upon me.

Thus we must attribute the characterization of Christ-Jesus, which we find in the first chapters of the Gospel of St. John as far as the end of the 10th Chapter, to the knowledge which might be possessed by any one who had not yet, in the deepest sense of the word, been initiated through Christ-Jesus Himself.

Now, you will say: "Yes, but we have already in these lectures listened to profound words about Christ-Jesus as the incarnated Logos, the Light of the World, etc." It is no longer surprising that these profound words concerning Christ-Jesus were spoken even in the very first Chapters, for in the ancient Mysteries, Christ-Jesus, who was to appear in the world at a future time, in other words, the Christ, was not perhaps an unknown being. And all the Mysteries point to One who was to come. For this reason the ancient initiates were called "prophets" because they prophesied concerning something that was to take place. Thus the purpose of initiation was to let it be clearly understood that in the future of mankind the Christ would be revealed, and in what he had already learned at that time, the Baptist found the truth which made it possible to state that He, who had been spoken of in the Mysteries, stood before him in the person of Christ-Jesus.

How all this is connected and what the relationship was between the so-called Baptist and Christ-Jesus will become clearer to us if we answer two questions. One of these questions is the following:— What was the position of the Baptist in his own age? The other leads back to the explanation of various passages at the beginning of the Gospel.

What was the position of the Baptist in his own age? Who, in fact, was the Baptist? He was one of those who—like others in their initiation —had received indications of the coming Christ, but he was represented as the only one to whom the true mystery concerning Christ-Jesus had been revealed, namely, that He who had appeared was the Christ Himself.

Those who were called Pharisees or were designated by other names saw in Christ-Jesus some one who in fact opposed their old principles of initiation, one who in their eyes did things to which they in their conservatism could not accede. Just because of their conservatism they said:—We must adhere to the old principles of initiation. And this inconsistency of constantly speaking about the future Christ, yet never admitting that the moment had arrived when He was really present, was the reason for their conservatism. Therefore when Christ-Jesus initiated Lazarus, they looked upon it as a violation of the ancient Mystery-traditions. "This man performs many signs! We can have no intercourse with him!" According to their understanding, He had betrayed the Mysteries, had made public what should be confined within their secret depths. Now we can see how to them this was like a betrayal and seemed to be a valid reason for rising up against Him. From that time, because of this, a change takes place; the persecution of Christ-Jesus begins.

How did the Baptist represent himself in the first chapters of this Gospel? In the first place, as one who was well acquainted with the Mystery-truths of the Christ Who was to come; as one who knew very well that the writer of the Gospel of St. John himself could repeat all that he, the Baptist, already knew, having become convinced of its truth through what we are now about to learn.

We have heard what the very first words of the Gospel mean. We shall now consider for a moment what is said there about the Baptist himself. Let us present it once more in the best possible translation. Thus far we have only heard the very first words:

In the beginning was the Word, and the Word was with God and the Word was a God.

The same was in the beginning with God.

All things came into being through It and save through It was not anything made that was made.

In It was Life and Life was the Light of men.

And the Light shone into the darkness but the darkness comprehended it not.

There was a man; he was sent from God, bearing the name John.

The same came as a witness in order to bear witness of the Light that through him all might believe.

He was not the Light but was a witness of the Light.

For the true Light which lighteth every man should come into the world.

It was in the world and the world came into being through It, but the world knew It not.

It entered into individual men (that is, the ego-men); but individual men (the ego-men) received it not.

But they who received it could reveal themselves as Children of God.

They who trusted in His name were not born of the blood, nor of the will of the flesh, nor of the will of man—but of God.

And the Word was made flesh and dwelt among us and we have heard His teaching, the teaching of the once born Son of the Father filled with Devotion and Truth.

John bare witness of Him and proclaimed clearly: He it was of whom I said:—He will come after me, who was before me. For He is my forerunner.

For out of His fullness have we all received Grace upon Grace.

For the law was given through Moses, but Grace and Truth came through Jesus-Christ.

Hitherto hath no one beheld God with his eyes. The once-born Son, who was in the bosom of the Universal-Father, has become the leader in this beholding.

These are the words which give again approximately the meaning of those first verses of the Gospel of St. John. However, before we come to their interpretation, we must add something else. How did John describe himself? You will remember that people were sent to discover who John the Baptist was. Priests and Levites came to him to ask him who he was. Why he gave the foregoing answer, we have yet to discover. Just at present we shall only consider what he said.

He said, "I am the voice of one calling in solitude." These are the words which stand there. "I am the voice of one calling in solitude." "In solitude" stands there quite literally. In Greek, the word *eremit* signifies the "solitary one." You can then understand that it is more correct to say, "I am the voice of one calling in solitude," than "I am the voice of one preaching in the wilderness." We shall better understand all that is presented in the opening words of the Gospel, if we call to mind John's own characterization of himself. Why does he call himself "the voice of one calling in solitude?"

We have seen that in the course of human evolution, the true Earth-mission is the evolution of love, but that love is only conceivable when it is given as a voluntary offering by self-conscious human beings. We have also seen that the human being little by little gains control of his ego and that slowly and gradually this ego sinks into human nature. We know that the animal, as such, has no individual ego. If the individual lion were able to say "I" to itself, the individual animal would not be meant thereby, but the group-ego in the astral world. All lions would say "I" to this group-ego. Thus whole groups of animals of like form say "I" to the supersensibly perceptible group-ego in the astral world. The great advantage human beings have over the animals is that of possessing an individual ego. The latter, however, only evolved by degrees, for human beings also began with a group-ego, with an ego belonging to a whole group of individuals.

If you were to go back to ancient peoples, to ancient races, you would find that originally human beings were everywhere formed into little groups. With the Germanic peoples you would not need to go very far back. In the writing of Tacitus it is quite evident that the German thought more of his whole tribe than of himself as an individual. The individual felt himself more as a member of the *Cheruskian* or of the *Sigambrian* tribe than as a separate personality. Therefore he partook of the fate of the whole tribe and when an individual member or the entire tribe received an affront, it did not matter who was the avenger.

Then in the course of time it happened that individual personalities gave up their tribal membership, and this resulted at last in the breaking up of the tribes so that they no longer held together. Human beings also evolved out of this group-soul characteristic and little by little they developed to a point where they could experience the ego in their own individual personalities. We can only understand certain things, especially religious documents, when we understand this mystery of the group-souls, of the group-egos. For those peoples who had come already to a certain conception of the individual ego, there still always existed a greater ego that spread out not only over groups living contemporaneously in a certain place, but also far beyond these groups. Human memory at the present time is of such a character that the individual remembers only his own youth. But there was a time when a different kind of memory existed, a time when the human being not only remembered his own deeds but also those of his father and of his grandfather as though they were his own. Memory reached out beyond birth and death as far as the blood relationship could be traced. The memory of an ancestor whose blood, as it were, flowed down through generations was preserved for centuries in this same blood, and a descendant or offspring of a tribe said "I" to the deeds and the thoughts of his forebears as though to himself. He did not feel himself limited by birth and death, but he felt himself as a member of a succession of generations, the central point of which was the ancestor. For what held the ego together was the fact that the individual remembered the deeds of the fathers and of the grandfathers. In ancient times this had its outer expression in the giving of names. The son remembered not only his own deeds but also those of his father and of his grandfather. Memory extended far back through generations and all that the memory thus encompassed was called in ancient times, for example, Noah or Adam. The individual human beings were not meant by these names, but the egos which for centuries had preserved the memory. This mystery was also concealed behind the names of the Patriarchs. Why did the Patriarchs live so long? It would never have occurred to the people of ancient times to denominate an individual human being by a special name during his life between birth and death. Adam was looked upon as a common memory, because the limits of time and space in ancient days played no part in the giving of names.

By degrees the human individual ego slowly freed itself from the group-soul, from the group-ego. The human being came gradually to a consciousness of his own individual ego. Formerly he felt his ego in his tribal membership, in the group of human beings to whom he was related through the blood tie, either as to time or space; hence the expression, "I and Father Abraham are one," which means one ego. The individual felt himself safe within the whole, because a common blood ran through the veins of all of the members of his particular people. Evolution progressed and the time became ripe for individuals right within their race to feel their own separate egos. It was the mission of the Christ to give to human beings what they needed in order that they might feel themselves secure and firm within their separate individual egos. In this way we should also interpret those words which can be so easily misunderstood namely, "He who does not deny wife and child, father and mother, brother and sister, cannot be my disciple!" We must not understand this in the trivial sense of instruction to run away from the family. But it means that every one should feel that he is an individual ego and that this individual ego is in direct union with the Spiritual Father who pervades the world. Formerly a follower of the Old Testament said, "I and Father Abraham are one," because the Ego felt itself resting within the blood relationship. At that moment this feeling of oneness with the Spiritual Father-Substance had to become independent; no longer should the blood relationship be a guarantee of membership in the whole, but the knowledge of the pure Spiritual Father-Principle in whom all are one.

Thus we are told in the Gospel of St. John that the Christ is the great bestower of the Impulse which gives to men what is needed to make them feel themselves forever within their own separate, individual egos. This is the transition from the Old Testament to the New, for the old had always something of a group-soul character in which one ego felt itself associated with the others, but in reality never felt either itself or the other egos. Instead, it experienced the folk or tribal ego within which they all had a common shelter.

What must be the feeling of an ego that has become so matured that it no longer feels the connection with the other individual personalities of the group-soul? What must have been the feelings of the individualized ego in a period in which it could be said: "The time is now past when union with other persons, union with all egos belonging to a group-soul can be felt as an actual life-reality; first, however, One must come who will give the spiritual Bread of Life to the soul from which the individual ego may receive nourishment." This separate ego had to feel itself solitary and the forerunner of the Christ was compelled to say: I am an ego that has broken away, that feels itself alone, and just because I have learned to feel solitary, I feel like a prophet to whom the ego gives real spiritual nourishment in solitude. Therefore the herald had to designate himself as one calling in solitude, which means the individual ego isolated from the group-soul calling for what can give it spiritual sustenance. "I am the voice of one calling in solitude." Thus we hear again the profound truth:—Each human individual ego is one wholly dependent upon itself; I am the voice of the ego that is freed, seeking a foundation upon which it, as an independent ego, can rest.—Now we understand the passage, "I am the voice of one calling in solitude."

In order that we may accurately understand the words of the Gospel, we shall need to familiarize ourselves a little with the way names and designations were then usually given. The giving of names at that time was not so abstract and devoid of meaning as it is at present, and if the exponents of biblical documents would only consider a little how much is expressed in this way, many trivial interpretations would never come to the light of day. I have already pointed out that when the Christ said, "I am the Light of the World," He really meant that He was the first to give expression to the "I AM" and was the Impulse for it. Therefore in the first chapters wherever "I AM" is to be found, it must be especially emphasized. All names and designations in ancient times in a certain sense are very real—yet at the same time they are used in a profoundly symbolical manner. This is often the source of tremendous errors made in two directions. From a superficial point of view, many say that according to such an interpretation a great deal is meant symbolically, but with such an explanation in which everything has only a symbolical meaning, they wish to have nothing to do, since historical, biblical events then disappear. On the other hand, those who understand nothing at all of the historical events may say:—"This is only meant symbolically." Those, however, who say such things, understand nothing of the Gospel. The historical reality is not denied because of a symbolic explanation, but it must be emphasized that the esoteric explanation includes both, the interpretation of the facts as historical and the symbolic meaning which we ascribe to them. Of course, if anyone sees only the prosaic external facts, namely, that a man was born somewhere, at some particular time, he will not understand that this man is something more than just a person with a particular name whose biography can be written. But whoever knows the spiritual relationship will learn to understand that besides being born in some particular place this living human being is also a symbol of his age and that what he signifies for the evolution of humanity is expressed in his name. It is something symbolic and historical at the same time, not

simply the one or the other. This is the important thing in a true interpretation of the Gospel. Therefore in almost all of the events and allu-
sions, we shall see that John—or the author of the Gospel bearing his name
—really has a supersensible perception; he sees at one and the same time
the outer events and the manifestation of deep spiritual truths. He has in
mind the historical figure of the Baptist; he is considering the historical
figure. But the true historical figure is for him at the same time a symbol
for all men who were in ancient times called upon to receive the imprint
of the Christ Impulse upon their egos, a symbol for those into whose
individual egos the Light of the World might shine, although they had
just started on the path. It was not, however, a symbol for those who in
their darkness were not yet able to apprehend the Light of the World.
What appeared as Life, Light, and Logos in Christ-Jesus, has always shone
in the world, but those who were first to become matured did not recognize it. The Light was always there, for had it not been there, the germ
of the ego could not possibly have come into existence.

Only the physical, ether and astral bodies of the present human being
existed within the Moon Evolution; there was no ego in them. Only
because the Light became transformed into that light which now shines
down upon the earth did It have the power to enkindle the individual
egos and to bring them gradually to maturity. "The Light shone in the
darkness but the darkness could not yet comprehend it." It entered into
the individual human being—right into the human ego—for an ego-
humanity could not have come into existence at all, had not the Light
been rayed into it by the Logos. However, ego-humanity as a whole did
not receive It, but only certain individuals, the initiates. They raised their
souls to the spiritual worlds and they always bore the name, "Children
of God," because they possessed knowledge of the Logos, of the Light, and
of Life and could always bear witness of These. There were certain ones
who already knew of the spiritual worlds through the ancient Mysteries.
What was present there in these initiates? It was the eternal human
living within them in full consciousness. In the mighty words, "I and the
Father are one," they felt, in fact, I and the great Primal Cause are one!
And the most profound thing of which they were conscious, their individual ego, they received not from father and mother but through their
initiation into the spiritual world. Not from the blood nor from the flesh

did they receive it, nor from the will of father or mother, but "from God," which means from the spiritual world.

Here we have an explanation of why it was that although the majority of mankind had already received the rudiments of an ego-being they could not as individuals receive the Light which had only descended, in fact, as far as the group-ego. Those, however, who received the Light—and they were few, indeed—could by means of it make themselves "Children of God." Those who put their trust in the Light were through initiation born of God. This gives us a clear picture. But in order that all men might perceive the living God, with their earthly senses, He, the Christ, had to appear upon earth in a way that made it possible for Him to be seen with physical eyes; in other words, He had to take on a form of flesh, because only such a form can be seen with physical eyes. Prior to this, only the initiates could perceive Him through the Mysteries, but now He took on a physical form for the salvation of every soul. "The Word or the Logos became flesh." Thus the writer of the Gospel of St. John links the historical appearance of Christ-Jesus together with the whole of evolution. "We have heard His teaching—the teaching of the once-born Son of the Father!" What manner of teaching is this? How were other men born?

In the ancient times in which the Gospels were written, those who were born of the flesh were called "twice-born." They were called twice-born—let us say—because of the intermingling of the blood of father and mother. Those who were not born of flesh and did not come into existence through a human act or through the mingling of blood, were "born of God," that is to say, they were "once-born." Those who were previously called "Children of God" were always in a certain sense the "once-born" and the teaching about the Son of God is the teaching of the "once-born." The physical man is "twice-born," the spiritual man is "once-born." You must not understand it to mean born into (*hineingeboren*)—no, "once-born" (*eingeboren*) is the antithesis of "twice-born" (*zweigeboren*). These words point to the fact that besides the physical birth, the human being can experience also a spiritual birth, namely, union with the Spirit, a birth through which he is "once-born," a child or a son of the Godhead.

Such a teaching had first to be heard from Him who represented the Word-made-Flesh. Through Him this teaching became general—"this teaching of the once-born Son of the Father, filled with Devotion and Truth." Devotion is the better translation here, because we have to do not only with being born out of the Godhead, but also with continued union with It, with the removal of all illusions which only come from being "twice-born" and which surround men with sense-deceptions. On the contrary it is a teaching, the truth of which is substantiated by Christ-Jesus Himself, living and dwelling among men as the incarnated Logos.

John the Baptist called himself—literally interpreted—the forerunner, the precursor, the one who goes before as herald of the ego. He designated himself as one who knew that this ego must become an independent entity in each individual soul, but he also had to bear witness of Him who was to come, in order that this be brought about. He said very clearly, "That which is to come is the 'I AM,' which is eternal, which can say of Itself, "Before Abraham was, was the I AM." John could say, "The I (the ego) which is spoken of here existed before me. Although I am Its forerunner, yet It is at the same time my Forerunner. I bear witness of what was previously present in every human being. After me will come One Who was before me."

At this point in the Gospel very significant words are spoken:—"For of His Fulness have we all received grace upon grace." There are men who call themselves Christians, who pass over this word, "Fulness," thinking that nothing very special is meant by it. "Pleroma" in Greek means "Fulness." We find this word also in the Gospel of St. John: "For from the Pleroma have we all received grace upon grace." I have said that if we wish really to understand this Gospel, every word must be weighed in the balance. What is then, Pleroma, Fulness? He alone can understand it who knows that in the ancient Mysteries Pleroma or Fulness was referred to as something very definite. For at that time it was already being taught that when those spiritual beings manifested themselves who during the Moon period evolved to the stage of divinity namely, the Elohim, one of them separated from the others. One remained behind upon the Moon, and thence *reflected* the power of Love until humanity was sufficiently matured to be able to receive the *direct* Light of the other six Elohim. Therefore they distinguished between Jahve, the individual God, the reflector, and the Fulness of the Godhead, "Pleroma," consisting of the other six Elohim. Since the full consciousness of the Sun Logos meant to them the Christ, they called Him the "Fulness of the Gods" when they wished to refer to Him. This profound truth was concealed in the words:—"For out of the Pleroma, we have received grace upon grace."

Now let us continue by transplanting ourselves back into the age of the group-souls, when each individual felt his own ego as the group-ego. Let us now consider what kind of a social organization existed in the group. As far as they were visible human beings, they lived as individuals. They felt inwardly the group-ego, but outwardly they were individuals. Since they did not yet feel themselves as separate entities, they were also unable yet to experience inner love to its fullest extent. One person loved another because he was related to him through blood. The blood relationship was the basis of all love. First those related by blood loved each other and all love, as far as it was not sex-love, sprang from this blood relationship. Men must free themselves more and more from this group-soul love and proffer love as a free gift of the ego. At the end of the earth evolution, a time will come for mankind when the ego, now become independent, will receive into its inner being, in full surrender, the impulse to do the right and good. Because the ego possesses this impulse, it will do the right and the good. When love becomes spiritualized to such a degree that no one will wish to follow any other impulse than this, then that will be fulfilled which Christ-Jesus wished to bring into the world. For one of the mysteries of Christianity is that it teaches the seeker to behold the Christ, to fill himself with the power of His image, to seek to become like Him, and to follow after Him. Then will his liberated ego need no other law; it will then, as a being free in its inner depths, do the good and the true. Thus Christ is the bringer of the impulse of freedom from the law, that good may be done, not because of the compulsion of any law, but as an indwelling Impulse of Love within the soul. This Impulse will still need the remainder of the Earth period for its full development. The beginning has been made through Christ-Jesus, and the Christ figure will always be the power which will educate humanity to it. As long as men were not yet ready to receive an independent ego, as long as they existed as members of a group, they had to be socially regulated by an outwardly revealed law. And even today men have not, in all things, risen above the group-egos. In how many things in the present are men not individual human beings, but group-beings? They are already trying to become free, but it is still only an ideal. (At a certain stage of esoteric discipleship, they are called the homeless ones.) The man who voluntarily places himself within the cosmic activities is an individual; he is not ruled by law. In the Christ Principle lies the victory over law. "For the law was given by Moses, but Grace through Christ." According to the Christian acceptation of the word, the soul's capacity for doing right out of the inner self was called Grace. Grace and an inner recognition of truth came into being through the Christ. You see how profoundly this thought fits into the whole of human evolution.

In earlier ages, those who were initiated developed higher spiritual organs of perception; previously no one ever saw God with physical eyes. The once-born Son who rests in the bosom of the Father is the first who made it possible for us to behold a God in the way we see a human being upon earth with the physical earthly senses. Previously God had remained invisible. He revealed Himself in the supersensible world through dreams or in other ways in the places of Initiation. Now God has become an historical fact, a form in the flesh. We read this in the words: "Before this no one had beheld God. The once-born Son who dwelt in the bosom of the Universal Father became the guide to this perceiving." He brought mankind to the point where it could behold God with earthly senses.

Thus we can see how sharply and clearly the Gospel of St. John points to the historical event of Palestine and in what exemplary and concise words which must be accurately weighed in the balance if we wish to use them for an understanding of Esoteric Christianity.

Now we shall see in the following lectures how this theme is further developed and at the same time how it is shown that the Christ is not only the guide of those who are united with the group-soul, but how He enters into each individual human being and endows the individual ego itself with His Impulse. The blood-tie indeed remains, but the spiritual aspect of love is added to it, and to this love which passes over from one individual, independent ego to another, He gives His Impulse.

Day by day, one truth after another was revealed to the neophyte in the course of his initiation. A very important truth is always disclosed, for example, on the third day. Then it is that one learns fully to understand that there is a point in the evolution of the earth when physical love, bound up with the blood, becomes ever more spiritualized. This point of time is the event which demonstrated the transition from a love dependent upon the blood-tie to a spiritualized form of love. In significant words Christ-Jesus makes reference to this when He says: "A time will come which is my time, a time when the most important things will no longer be accomplished by men bound by the tie of blood, but by those who stand alone by themselves. This time however is yet to come." The Christ Himself who gave the first impulse, says on one important occasion that this ideal will sometime be fulfilled, but that His time is not yet come. He prophetically points to this when His mother stands there and asks Him to do something for mankind, hinting that she has the right to induce Him to an important deed for humanity. He then replies, "What we are able to do today is still connected with the blood bond, with the relationship between thee and me, for My time is not yet come." That such a time will come when each must stand alone is expressed in the narrative of the Marriage at Cana when the announcement: "They have no wine," was answered by Jesus with the words: "That is something that has still to do with *thee and me,* for My time is not yet come." Here we have the words, "between thee and me" and "My time is not yet come." What stands there in the text refers to this mystery. Like many others, this passage also is usually very roughly translated. It should not read: "Woman, what have I to do with thee?" but: "This has to do with me and thy blood relationship." The text is very fine and subtle, but comprehensible only to those who have the will to understand it. But when, in our age, these religious documents are repeatedly interpreted by all kinds of people, one would like to ask, have those who call themselves Christians then no feeling for all this, that they make the Christ utter the words, incorrectly translated, "Woman, what have I to do with thee?"

In much that today calls itself Christianity which rests upon the teaching of the Gospel, we are inclined to ask, *Do they really possess the Gospel?* The important thing is that *they should first possess it.* And with such a profound document as the Gospel of St. John every word must be weighed in order that its proper value be recognized.

V

THE SEVEN DEGREES OF INITIATION

The First Sign

In a consideration of the Gospel of St. John, we should never lose sight of that most important point which was brought out in the lecture yesterday namely, that in the original writer of the Gospel we have to do with the "Beloved Disciple," initiated by Christ-Jesus Himself. One might naturally ask if, aside from occult knowledge, there exists, perhaps, some external proof of this statement by means of which the writer of this Gospel has intimated that he came to a higher order of knowledge about the Christ through the "raising," through the initiation which is represented in the so-called miracle of the raising of Lazarus. If you will read the Gospel of St. John carefully, you will observe, that nowhere previous to that chapter which treats of the raising of Lazarus is there any mention of the "Disciple whom the Lord loved." In other words, the real author of the Gospel wishes to say: What precedes this chapter does not yet have its origin in the knowledge which I have received through initiation, therefore in the beginning you must disregard me. Only later does he mention the "Disciple whom the Lord loved." Thus the Gospel falls into two important parts, the first part in which the Disciple whom the Lord loved is not yet mentioned because he had not yet been initiated, and that part which comes after the raising of Lazarus in which this Disciple is mentioned. Nowhere in the document itself will you find any contradictions of what I have presented in the previous lectures. Naturally, anyone who considers the Gospel only superficially will easily pass this by, will not notice it and at the present time when everything is popularized, when all manner of knowledge is forced upon us, we can often experience as an extraordinary spectacle much of a very doubtful character in this knowledge.

Who would not consider it a blessing if all kinds of knowledge could be brought to the people through such inexpensive literature as the *Reclam'sche Universal Bibliothek*. Among the last volumes, one has appeared on the *Origin of the Bible*. The author entitles himself a Doctor

78

of Theology. He is, then, a theologian! He believes that throughout all the chapters of the Gospel of St. John, from the 35th verse of the 1st Chapter, John, the author of the Gospel, is the one referred to. When this little book came into my hands, I really could not believe my eyes and said to myself: there must be something very extraordinary under consideration here that repudiates all previous occult points of view that the Beloved Disciple is not mentioned before the "raising of Lazarus." Still, a theologian ought to know! In order not to pass judgment too quickly, take up the Gospel of St. John and see for yourselves what stands there: "Again the next day after, John stood and two of his disciples." Here John the Baptist and two of his disciples are spoken of. The most generous point of view that one can take toward this theologian is that his consciousness was filled with an ancient exoteric tradition which declares that John, the author of the Gospel, is one of these two disciples. This tradition is supported by Matthew IV 21. But, the Gospel of St. John cannot be explained by means of the other Gospels. A theologian therefore was responsible for introducing into popular literature a very harmful book. And if one knows how such a thing which is brought to the people in just this way continues to spread, it is possible to measure the harm which arises out of it. This is just an interpellation, in order that a certain protective wall may be erected against all kinds of objections which might perhaps be brought forward in refutation of what has been said here.

Now let us hold in mind that what preceded the "raising of Lazarus" is a communication of weighty matters, but that the writer has reserved the most profound matters for the chapters subsequent to that event. Nevertheless, he wished throughout to indicate that the content of his Gospel is something which will be thoroughly understood only by one who has attained a certain degree of initiation. Therefore he indicates in various passages that what is communicated in the first chapters has to do with a certain kind and degree of initiation. You already know that there are different degrees of initiation. For example, in a certain form of oriental initiation, seven degrees can be distinguished and these seven degrees were designated by all sorts of symbolical names. The first was the degree of the "Raven," the second that of the "Occultist," the third of the "Warrior," the fourth that of the "Lion." Amongst different peoples, who still felt a kind of blood relationship as the expression of their group-soul, the fifth degree was designated by the name of the folk itself; thus among the Persians, for example, an initiate of the fifth degree was called in an occult sense, a "Persian." When we understand what these names signify, then the justification of these titles will soon be evident.

An initiate of the first degree is one who constitutes an intermediary between the hidden and the outer life, one who is sent from place to place. In this first degree the neophyte must devote himself with complete resignation to the outer life, but what he ascertains there, he must bring back into the Mystery Places. One speaks of the "Raven" when words have something to communicate to the inner world of the Mystery Places from the world outside. Just call to mind the ravens of Elias, or the ravens of Wotan, even the ravens of the Barbarossa Saga, that had to discover when it was time to come forth. The initiate of the second degree stood fully within the occult life. One who was of the third degree was allowed to defend occult knowledge. The degree of the "Warrior" does not mean one who fights, but one who defends occult teaching, what the occult life has to give. One who is a "Lion" embodies the occult life within himself in such a way that he defends occultism, not only in words, but also in acts, that is, with deeds of a magical sort. The sixth degree is that of the "Sun-hero" and the seventh that of the "Father". The fifth degree is the one we shall now consider.

The human being of ancient times was especially a part of his community and therefore when he was conscious of his ego, he felt himself more as a member of a group-soul than as an individual. But the initiate of the fifth degree had made a certain sacrifice, had so far stripped off his own personality that he took the folk-soul into his own being. While other men felt their souls within the folk-soul, he took the folk-soul into his own being, and this was because all that belonged to his personality was of no importance to him but only the common folk-spirit. Therefore an initiate of this kind was called by the name of his particular folk.

Now we know that in the Gospel of St. John it is said that Nathaniel also was one of the first disciples of Christ-Jesus. He was brought before the Christ. He is not so highly developed that he is able to comprehend the Christ. The Christ is, of course, the Spirit of all-inclusive Knowledge which cannot be fathomed by a Nathaniel, an initiate of the fifth degree. But the Christ could fathom Nathaniel. This was shown by two facts.

How did Christ designate him? "This man is a true Israelite!" Here
we have the designation according to the name of the folk. Just as among
the Persians, an initiate of the fifth degree is called a Persian, so among
the Israelites, he is called an Israelite. Therefore Christ calls Nathaniel
an Israelite. He then says to him: "Even before Philip called thee, when
thou wast under the fig-tree, I saw thee!" That is a symbolical designation
of an initiate like the Budha sitting under the Bodhi Tree. The fig-tree
is a symbol of Egyptian-Chaldean initiation. He meant with these words:
I well know that thou art an initiate of a certain degree, and canst perceive certain things, for I saw thee! Then Nathaniel recognized Him:
"Rabbi, Thou art the Son of God; Thou art the King of Israel!" This
word "King" signifies in this connection: Thou art one who is higher
than I, otherwise thou couldst not say, "I saw thee when thou sattest under
the fig-tree." And Christ answered, "Thou believest in me because I said
that I saw thee under the fig-tree: thou shalt see greater things than
these." The words "verily, verily" we shall speak about later. Then He
said: "I say unto you, ye shall see the angels of Heaven ascending and
descending upon the Son of Man." Yet greater things than they had
already seen would be seen by those who were able to recognize the Christ.
Again, one may ask: What significant words are these?

In order to make this clear, let us call to mind what the human being
really is. We have said that he is a different creature by day than by night.
During the day his four human members, physical body, ether body,
astral body, and ego are bound closely together. They react upon each
other. We may say that when the human being is awake during the day,
in a certain way his physical and etheric bodily parts are permeated and
cared for by his astral and ego spiritual parts. But we have also shown
that something else must be active within the etheric and physical bodily
parts in order that the human being be able to exist at all in his present
phase of evolution. For we have called attention to the fact that every
night he draws out those members which care for this physical and ether
body, namely, the astral body and ego, thus leaving his physical and ether
bodies to their own fate. You all, as astral body and ego, faithlessly desert
your physical and ether bodies every night. Hence you will see that
Spiritual Science points out with a certain correctness that divine-spiritual
powers and forces stream through the physical and ether bodies during

the night so that they are, as it were, invested by these divine-spiritual forces and beings. We have also pointed out that when the astral body and ego were outside the physical and ether bodies in those periods which we call the Jahve or Jehova epochs, that Jehova was active as an inspirer. But it was the true Light, the Fullness of the Godhead or of the Elohim, the Pleroma, that was also constantly radiating through the physical and ether bodies. However, the human being, not having yet received the necessary impulse from the Christ-principle before the appearance of this Principle upon the earth, was not able to recognize it. Those principles which are to come to expression in the physical body, dwell in the higher spiritual regions of Devachan. The spiritual beings and powers which work upon the physical body are at home in the higher heavenly spheres, in higher Devachan, and those powers which work upon the ether body are in their own sphere in the lower heavenly realms. So we may say that in this physical body there are constantly active, beings from the highest regions of Devachan and in the ether body, beings from the lower devachanic regions are active. Men can recognize them only after having received the Impulse of the Christ into themselves. "If you truly understand the Son of Man, you will perceive how the spiritual forces descending from and ascending to the heavenly spheres work upon mankind. This you will know through the impulse which the Christ gives to the earth."

What now follows, was mentioned in the lecture yesterday. The Marriage at Cana in Galilee is often called "the first of the miracles"—it were better to call it "the first sign" which Christ-Jesus made. Now in order that we may understand the stupendousness of the significance of the Marriage at Cana, we shall need to consider as a whole, much of what we have been hearing in the last lectures.

In the first place we have here a marriage—but why a marriage in Galilee? We shall understand why it is a marriage in Galilee if we call to mind once more the whole mission of the Christ. His mission consisted in bringing to mankind the full force of the ego, an inner independence in the soul. The individual ego should feel itself fully independent and separate, existing completely within itself and people should be united in marriage because of a love which they freely and voluntarily bestow upon one another. Through the Christ-Principle there should come into the earth-mission a love that would rise ever higher and higher above the material and constantly mount toward the Spirit. Love had its beginning in its lowest form which was bound up with the senses. In the earliest periods of human evolution, those who were bound together by the tie of blood loved each other and they made a great deal of the idea that love was based upon this material blood relationship.

The Christ came in order to spiritualize this love; in order, on the one hand, to loosen the bonds in which love had been entangled through the blood-relationship and on the other hand to give force and intensity to *spiritual* Love. Among the followers of the Old Testament we still see expressed most completely what we may call membership in the group-soul acting as the foundation of the individual ego within the Universal Ego. We have seen that the expression "I and Father Abraham are one" had a definite meaning for the adherents of the Old Testament. It meant that they felt themselves safe in the consciousness that that blood which ran through the veins of Father Abraham flowed on down even to them, selves. Therefore they felt themselves secure within the whole and only those were considered members of the whole who came into being through human propagation maintained by means of this blood relationship. In the very beginning of human evolution upon the earth, marriage took place only within very narrow circles, within families related by blood. Endogamy, (marriage within the tribe) was closely adhered to. Then the narrow blood-circle gradually widened and men began to marry outside the family, but not yet within other peoples or folk. The folk of the Old Testament held fast to the idea that the folk blood relationship should be maintained. One is a "Jew" who in his blood is a Jew.

Christ Jesus did not advocate this principle. He appealed to those who had broken this principle of mere blood relationship, and the important thing He had to demonstrate, He demonstrated not in Judea, but outside in Galilee. Galilee was the region where peoples of every race and tribe had mixed together. The term Galilean means "mixed-breed," "mongrel." Christ Jesus went to the Galileans, to those who were most mixed. Out of a human reproduction such as this, brought about by a mingling of blood, something arose that was no longer dependent upon a physical basis of love. Therefore what He wished to say, was said at a marriage. But why at a marriage? Because at the time of a marriage reference can be made to the reproduction of human beings. And what He wished to demonstrate, He did not wish to show at a place where marriage took place within narrow boundaries, within the blood-bond, but where it was entered into independently of the tie of blood. Therefore what He had to say was said at a marriage— and at a marriage in Galilee. If we wish to understand what is expressed here, we must again turn our attention to the whole of human evolution.

It has often been said that for the occultist there is no such thing as the merely external, the purely material. All materiality is for him the expression of something of a soul-spirit nature, and just as your face is the expression of something of a soul-spirit nature, so too is the light of the sun the expression of a soul-spirit light. All that occurs apparently only in the material physical world is at the same time the expression of deeper spiritual processes. Occultism does not deny matter. For it, even the grossest matter is the expression of a soul-spirit something. Thus material facts correspond to the spiritual evolutionary processes of the world, always running parallel with them.

If in spirit we look back over human evolution to the time when mankind still lived upon an ancient Continent lying between Europe and America, upon ancient Atlantis, passing over from there into the later post-Atlantean period, we can see how generation after generation has at last led right up to ourselves. If we consider from the standpoint of race the whole significance of human evolution from the 4th to the 5th Root-race, we can see, as it were, that out of an Atlantean humanity, wholly or completely immersed in the group-soul, the individual ego of the human personality gradually evolved and slowly matured in the post-Atlantean period. What the Christ brought spiritually through His powerful spiritual impulse had to be prepared gradually through other impulses. What Jahve did was to implant the group-soul ego in the astral body and by gradually maturing it, prepare it for the reception of the fully independent "I AM." But men could only comprehend this "I AM" when their physical body also became a fit instrument for sheltering It. You can easily imagine that the astral body might be ever so capable of receiving an ego, but if the physical body is not a fit instrument for truly comprehending the "I AM" with a waking consciousness then it is impossible to receive it. The physical body must also always be a suitable instrument for what is imprinted upon it here upon the earth. Therefore when the astral body had been matured, the physical body had to be prepared to become an instrument of the "I AM," and this is what occurred in human evolution. We can follow the processes through which the physical body was prepared to become the bearer of the self-conscious, ego-endowed human being.

Even in the Bible it is pointed out that Noah who, in a certain sense was the progenitor of his race in the post-Atlantean period, was the first wine-drinker, the first to experience the effect of alcohol. Then we come to a chapter which may be really very shocking for many people. In the post-Atlantean period an extraordinary cultus arose; this was the worship of Dionysos. You all know that this worship was connected with wine. This extraordinary substance was first introduced to human beings in the post-Atlantean period and produced a certain effect upon them. You know that every substance has some effect upon the human creature and alcohol had a very definite action upon the human organism. In fact, in the course of human evolution, it has had a mission. Strange as it may seem, it has had the task, as it were, of preparing the human body so that it might be cut off from connection with the Divine, in order to allow the personal "I AM" to emerge. Alcohol has the effect of severing the connection of the human being with the spirit world in which he previously existed. It still has this effect today. It was not without reason that alcohol has had a place in human evolution. In the future of humanity, it will be possible to see in the fullest sense of the word that it was the mission of alcohol to draw men so deeply into materiality that they become egoistic, thus bringing them to the point of claiming the ego for themselves, no longer placing it at the service of the whole folk. Alcohol performed a service, the contrary of the one performed by the human group-soul. It deprived men of the capacity to feel themselves at one with the whole in the spirit world. Hence the Dionysian worship which cultivated a living together in a kind of external intoxication, a merging into the whole without observing this whole. Evolution in the post-Atlantean period has been connected with the worship of Dionysos, because this worship was a symbol of the function and mission of alcohol. Now, when mankind is again endeavouring to find its way back, when the ego has been so far developed that the human being is again able to find union with the divine spiritual powers, the time has come for a certain reaction, an unconscious one at first, to take place against alcohol. This reaction is now taking place and many persons today already feel that something which once had a very special significance is not forever justified.

No one should interpret what has been said concerning the mission of alcohol at a special period of time as, perhaps, favoring alcohol, but it should be understood that this has been stated in order to make clear that this alcoholic mission has been fulfilled and that different things are adapted to different periods. In the same period in which men were drawn most deeply into egotism through alcohol, there appeared a force stronger than all others which could give to them the greatest impulse for re-finding a union with the spiritual whole. On the one hand men had to descend to the lowest level in order that they might become independent and on the other hand a strong force must come which can give again the impulse for finding the path back to the Universal. The Christ indicated this to be His mission in the first of His signs. In the first place He had to point out that the ego must become independent; in the second place, that He was addressing Himself to those who had freed themselves from the blood relationship. He had to turn to a marriage where the physical bodies came under the influence of alcohol, because at this marriage wine would be drunk. And Christ Jesus showed how His mission had to proceed in the different earthly epochs. How often we hear extraordinary explanations of the meaning of the changing of water into wine. Even from the pulpit one hears that nothing else is meant than that the insipid water of the Old Testament should be superceded by the strong wine of the New. In all probability it was the wine-lovers who always liked this kind of an explanation, but these symbols are not so simple as that. It must be kept constantly in mind that the Christ said: My mission is one that points toward the far distant future when men will be brought to a union with the Godhead—that is to a love of the Godhead as a free gift of the independent ego. This love should bind men in freedom to the Godhead while formerly an inner compelling impulse of the group-soul had made them a part of It.

Let us now grasp in accordance with the prevailing thought of that time what men then experienced. Let us especially understand the thoughts that they held. It was declared that people were at one time united with the group-soul and felt their union with the Godhead. Then they developed a downward tendency and this was considered as an entanglement in matter, as a degeneration, a kind of falling away from the Divine, and the question was asked: whence came originally what the human being now possesses? From what has he fallen away? The further we go back in earthly evolution, the more we find the solid, earthly matter passing over into a fluidic state under the influence of warmer conditions. But we know that when the earth was much more fluidic than it became later on, human beings also existed, but they were much less detached from the Godhead than at a subsequent period. To the degree that the earth hardened, human things became materialized. At the time the earth was in a fluidic condition, the human being was contained within the watery element, but he could only walk about upon the earth after it had already deposited solid portions. Therefore, people felt the hardening of the physical body and could say: the human being was born out of the earth when it was still in its fluidic state, but at that time he was still wholly united with the Godhead. All that brought him into matter defiled him. Those who are to remember this ancient connection with the Divine were baptized with water. This was its symbol: Let yourself become conscious of your ancient union with the Godhead, conscious that you have become defiled, that you have descended to your present condition.

The Baptist also baptized in this way in order to bring mankind into a closer union with the Godhead. And this is what all baptism signified in ancient times. It is a radical expression, but one which brings to our consciousness what is meant. Christ Jesus had to baptize with something different. He had to direct men, not to the past, but to the future through the development of a spirituality in their inner being. Through the "holy", the undimmed and undefiled Spirit, the human spirit could be united with the Godhead. Baptism by water was a baptism of remembrance, that of the Holy Spirit is one of prophecy pointing to the future. That relationship which has been wholly lost, and which baptism by water recalls to mind has also been lost in all that was expressed in the symbol of the wine, of the sacrificial wine. Dionysos was the dismembered God who was drawn into the individual souls, separate parts no longer knowing anything of one another. Humanity was split into many pieces and thrown into matter through what alcohol has brought to the world, alcohol the symbol of Dionysos. In the Marriage at Cana, a great principle was preserved, the instructive principle of evolution. There are, to be sure, absolute truths, but they cannot at all times be revealed to men without preparation. Each age must have its special function, its special truths. Why is it that we can speak today of reincarnation, etc.? Why are we able to sit together in such an assembly as this and foster Spiritual Science? We can do so, because all of the souls which are present within you today have been incarnated upon the earth in so and so many bodies and so and so many times. Very many of the souls which are within you now lived at one time in the Germanic countries where the Druid priests walked among you and brought to your souls Spiritual Wisdom in the form of myth and saga. And because your soul received it in that form at that time, it is now in the position to receive it in another form, the Anthroposophical. At that time it was in the form of pictures—today it is in the form of Anthroposophy. But then it would not have been possible to impart truth in its present form. Do not imagine that the ancient Druid priest would have been able to impart the truth in the form in which it is presented today. Anthroposophy is the form befitting the humanity of the present or of the immediate future. In later incarnations truth will be proclaimed, and men will work for it in quite different forms, and what is now called Anthroposophy will be related as something remembered, just as we now relate the Sagas and Fairy-tales. Anthroposophists should not be foolish enough to say that in ancient times there existed only stupidities and childish ideas, and that we alone have advanced the world so gloriously. Those, for example, who pretend to be monists do this. But we are working in Spiritual Science in preparation for the next epoch. For if our present age were not here, the next would likewise not come. No one should, however, make the future an excuse for present conduct. Much nonsense is indulged in also in respect of the teaching of Reincarnation. I have met people who said that in their present incarnation they did not need to be respectable human beings, because for this they had time enough later on. If, however, one does not begin with it today, the consequences will appear straightway in the next incarnation.

So we must understand clearly that there is nothing absolutely fixed in the forms of truth, but that what corresponds to a particular epoch of human evolution, always becomes known. That greatest impulse of evolution had, as it were, to descend even into the life customs of that time. For it had to clothe the highest truth in language and functions befitting the understanding of the particular period in question. Therefore by means of a kind of Dionysian rite or wine sacrifice, the Christ had to tell how mankind could raise itself to the Godhead. One should not fanatically ask why Christ changed the water into wine. The age should be taken into consideration. Through a sort of Dionysian rite, Christ had to prepare for what was to come.

Christ goes to the Galileans who are jumbled together out of all kinds of nationalities that were not bound by the blood-tie and there He performed the first Sign of His mission and He adapted Himself so fully to their habits of life that he turned water into wine for them. Let us hold clearly in mind what the Christ really wished to say by this: Those who have descended to the stage of materialism, symbolized by the drinking of wine, will I also lead to a union with the Spirit.—So He will be there, not alone for those who can be raised by means of the symbol of baptism, by water. It is very significant that we are shown at once that here are six vessels of purification. We shall return to this number. Purification is what is accomplished by means of baptism. If in those epochs in which the Gospel had its origin one wished to express the fact of baptism, it was spoken of as a purification. The word "baptism" was never actually used, but they said "to-baptize", and what resulted through baptism was called "purification." Never will you find in the Gospel of St. John the corresponding βαπτίζω, except in verb form. But when it is used as a noun, it is the cleansing that is always meant, the process through which the human being is reminded of his state of purification, his relationship with the Godhead.

Even to the symbolical vessels of the rite of purification, Christ-Jesus undertook the Sign through which He indicated His mission as far as it was possible at that time. Thus in the marriage at Cana in Galilee, something of the profound mission of the Christ is expressed. He said: "My time will come in the future, it is not yet come. What I have to accomplish here has to do in part with what must be overcome through My mission." He stands in the present and at the same time points to the future, thereby showing how He works for the age, not in an absolute but in a cultural, educational sense. It is the mother, therefore, who besought Him and said, "They have no wine." But He replied: "What I have now to accomplish has still to do with ancient times, with *me and thee,* for My proper time has not yet come when wine will be transformed back again into water." How could it have had any meaning at all to say, "Woman, what have I to do with thee?" when He then complied with what the mother had asked! It only has a meaning if we are shown that the present condition of humanity has been brought about because of the blood relationship and that a Sign has been performed in accordance with ancient usages which still needs the employment of alcohol in order to point to the time when the independent ego shall have risen above the tie of the blood; it has a significance only when we are shown that for the present we must still reckon with ancient times which are symbolized by wine, but that a later time is coming which will be "His time."

And chapter after chapter of the Gospel reveals to us two things. First it shows that what was communicated was for those who, in a certain way, were able to comprehend occult truths. In our times, exoteric Spiritual Science is presented in lectures, but at that period spiritual-scientific truths could only be understood by those who had been in a certain way actually initiated into this or that degree. Who were those who were able to understand something of what Christ-Jesus was saying about profound truths? Only those who were able to perceive outside of the physical body—those who could withdraw from the body and become conscious in the spirit world. If Christ-Jesus wished to speak to those who could understand Him, it had to be to those who were in a certain way initiated, those who could see spiritually. When, for example, He speaks of the re-birth of the soul in the chapter concerning His conversation with Nicodemus, we see that He is revealing these truths to someone who perceives with spiritual senses. You only need to read the following words:—

But there was a man of the Pharisees, named Nicodemus, a ruler of the Jews; the same came to Jesus *by night.*

Let us accustom ourselves to accuracy in dealing with words. We are told that Nicodemus came to Jesus "by night;" this means that he received

outside of the physical body what Christ-Jesus had to communicate to him. "By night" means that when he makes use of his spiritual senses, he comes to Christ-Jesus. Just as in their conversation about the fig-tree, Nathaniel and Christ-Jesus understood one another as initiates, so too a faculty of understanding is indicated here also.

The second thing shown us in the Gospel is that Christ has always a mission to perform that has nothing to do with the mere blood tie. That is very clearly shown by His approaching the Samaritan woman at the well. He gave her the instructions which He gave those whose ego had been lifted above the common blood tie:

Then cometh He to a city of Samaria which is called Sychar, near to the parcel of ground that Jacob gave to his son Joseph.

Now Jacob's well was there. Jesus, therefore, being wearied with His journey, sat thus on the well: and it was about the sixth hour.

There cometh a woman of Samaria to draw water: Jesus saith unto her, "Give me to drink," for His disciples were gone away into the city to buy meat.

Then saith the woman of Samaria unto Him, "How is it that thou, being a Jew, asketh drink of me, which am a woman of Samaria, for the Jews have no dealings with the Samaritans."

Here is indicated that it was something very strange that Christ should go to a people whose egos had been withdrawn, uprooted from the group-soul. That is the important thing.

In the narrative about the nobleman, we read further that the Christ not only breaks the bond of blood that binds men together in a marriage within the folk, but he breaks also that bond that separates them into classes. He came to those whose ego had been uprooted. He healed the son of the nobleman who, according to the interpretation of the Jews, was a stranger to Him. Throughout the Gospel it is pointed out that Christ is the missionary of the independent ego which is present in every human individual. Therefore, He could say:—"When I speak of Myself in a higher sense, of the I AM, I do not at all refer to my own ego residing within me, but to a being, to something which *everyone* possesses within himself. My ego is one with the Father, but in general the ego present in every personality is also one with the Father." That is also the deeper

meaning of the instructions which the Christ gave to the Samaritan woman at the well.

I should like to call your attention especially to a passage, which if rightly understood will enable you to come to a deep understanding. It is the passage from the 31st to the 34th verse of the 3rd chapter which naturally must be read so that the reader is conscious of its being John the Baptist who speaks these words:—

> He that cometh from above is above all: he that is of the earth is earthly and speaketh of the earth; he that cometh from heaven is above all. And what he hath seen and heard, to that he testifieth: and no man receiveth his testimony.
>
> But he that hath received his testimony hath set his seal that God is true.
>
> For he whom God hath sent speaketh the words of God: for God giveth not the Spirit by measure unto him.

I should like to meet anyone who understands these words according to this translation. What a contradiction! "He whom God hath sent, speaketh the word of God, for God giveth not the Spirit by measure unto him." What is the sense of these words?

In countless utterances, Christ says: "When I speak of *the* Ego, I speak of the Eternal Ego in men which is one with the spiritual foundations of the world. When I speak of *this* Ego, I speak of something which dwells in the innermost depths of the human soul. If any man hears Me (and now He is speaking only of the lower ego which feels nothing of the Eternal) he receiveth not My testimony. He understands nothing of what I say, for I can speak of nothing that flows from Me to him. Otherwise he would not then be independent. Every one must find within himself as his own eternal base, the God which I proclaim." A few verses back we find the passage:—

> And John also was baptizing in Enon near to Salim, because there was much water there: and they came and were baptized.
>
> Then there arose a question between some of John's disciples and the Jews about purification (this means about the form of baptism).

When such a question was raised in these circles, they were always speaking of the union with the Divine and of the submersion of humanity into

matter and of how, according to the old idea of God, union with the Divine took place through the group-soul. Thus others came and said to John: "Jesus also baptizes!" And John had to make it clear to them that what had come into the world through Jesus was something very special and this he did by saying that Jesus does not teach that union symbolized by the ancient form of baptism, but teaches how men will be their own guides through the free gift of the now independent ego. And each individual must discover the "I AM," the God, within himself. Only in this way is he in the position to find the Divine in his inner being. If these words are read thus, then the reader will be aware that He, the "I AM," was sent from God. He who was sent from God, who was sent to enkindle the Divine in this way, also preached God in the true sense, no longer according to the blood tie.

Let us translate these passages according to their true meaning, for we have now the basis for such a translation, if we understand how the teachings of the ancients were presented. They were poetically portrayed in many books. We need only recall the Psalms of the Old Testament where in beautifully constructed language, the Divine was proclaimed. At that time the ancient blood-relationship was spoken of only as a relationship with a God. This could all be learned, but all that was learned through it was nothing more than that one was related to this ancient divinity. But, if there was a desire to comprehend the Christ, then all the ancient laws, all the ancient artificialities were unnecessary. What the Christ taught could be understood to the degree that men understood the spiritual ego within themselves. At that time, it is true, it was not possible to have full knowledge of Divinity, but one could understand what was heard from the lips of Christ-Jesus. The preliminary conditions for understanding were there. The Psalms were not then necessary, nor all the poetically constructed teachings, for all that was needed was the simplest means of expression. One needed only to speak in halting words to become a witness of God. Even in the simplest, stammering words it was possible to become a witness of the Divine; it need be only single words without metre. Anyone who felt in his ego that he was sent from God, even though he were halting in his speech, could understand the words of the Christ. Anyone knowing only the earthly relationship with God speaks in the poetic measure of the Psalms, but all his metre leads him to nothing but the ancient gods. However, anyone who felt himself deeply rooted in the spirit worlds is above all, and can bear witness of what has been seen and heard in those worlds. But those who accepted a testimony only in the accustomed way did not accept His. If there were those who accepted it, they showed by their acceptance that they felt themselves sent from God. They not only *believed*, they *understood* what the other one said to them, and through their understanding they bore witness of their words. "He who feels the ego, reveals even in his stammering words the Word of God." This is what is meant, for the spirit here referred to does not need to express itself in metre, in any form of syllabic measure, but it can declare itself in the simplest, halting manner. Such words can easily be taken as a license for folly. But whoever refuses wisdom just because, in his opinion, the most sublime mysteries should be expressed in the simplest form possible, does so, although often quite unconsciously, merely from an inclination toward psychic ease. When it is said, "God giveth not the spirit by measure" (metre), it only means that the "measure" or metre does not help towards the spirit. But where the spirit really exists, there also is "measure". Not everyone who has "measure" has the "spirit"; but one who has the "spirit" will come most certainly to "measure" or metre. Naturally, certain things cannot be reversed. It is not an evidence of possessing the "spirit" if one has *no* "measure"; nor is the possession of "measure" a proof of the "spirit". Science is certainly no sign of wisdom, nor is a lack of science a proof of it.

So we are shown that Christ appeals to the independent ego in every human soul. "Measure" you must consider here as metre, *poetically constructed speech.* Then the foregoing sentence will read: "He who finds God in the 'I AM,' bears witness of Divine Speech or *God's language,* even in his stammering words"—and he finds the way to God.

VI

THE "I AM"

We have already pointed out in these lectures that in the words of Christ-Jesus to Nicodemus, we must recognize a conversation between Christ and a personality who is able to perceive what can be beheld outside of the physical body by means of higher organs of cognition if developed to a certain stage. For those who understand such things, this is clearly and distinctly indicated in the Gospel wherein it is stated that Nicodemus came to Christ-Jesus "in the night," meaning in a state of consciousness in which the human being does not make use of his outer sense organs. We shall not enter into the trivial explanations which have been presented by different people concerning these words, "in the night." You know that in this conversation the problem is one of rebirth of the human being "out of water and Spirit." These are very important words concerning rebirth which the Christ speaks to Nicodemus in the 4th verse of the 3rd Chapter:

Nicodemus said unto Him:—How can a man be reborn when he is old?

Jesus answered:—Verily, verily, I say unto thee, except a man be born of water and the spirit, he cannot enter into the Kingdom of God.

We have already said that these words must be carefully weighed and we should keep definitely in mind that the words of a religious document of this kind must be taken in a literal sense on the one hand, but on the other we must first discover and understand this literal meaning. The words are often quoted, "The letter killeth, but the spirit giveth life!" Those who quote these words often employ them in a very peculiar manner. They find in them a license for reading into them their own phantasy, which they call the "spirit of the thing," and then they say to someone who has taken the trouble to learn the letter before coming to the spirit: "What have we to do with the letter? The letter killeth, but the spirit giveth life." One who speaks in this manner, stands about on the same level with a man who would say: "The spirit is what truly lives, but the body is something dead. Therefore let us destroy the body, then will the spirit become alive." Whoever speaks in this way does not know that the spirit is formed gradually, that the human being must use the organs of his physical body for reception of what he experiences in the physical world, which he then raises into spirit. First we must know the letter, then we can kill it; likewise, when the spirit has drawn everything it can out of the human body, the latter falls away from the human spirit.

There is something extraordinarily profound just in this very chapter of the Gospel of St. John. We can only enter into the meaning of it, when we follow human evolution still further back than we have already in our consideration of the Gospel up to the present. Today we must trace the human being back into still more remote periods of the earth's evolution.

In order that you may not, at the very beginning, be too much shocked at what I shall have to say about these early human states, I should like to lead you back once more to the ancient Atlantean epoch.

We have already called attention to the fact that before that great cataclysm of our earth, a memory of which is retained in the sagas of the Flood, our human progenitors lived out there in the west in a region which no longer exists, but which now forms the bed of the Atlantic Ocean. This continent which is called the ancient Atlantis harbored our forefathers. When we examine the later epochs of this Atlantean period of human evolution, we find, even in these epochs of the far distant past, that at least the form of the human being was not so very much unlike his present one. However, if we should go back to the earliest periods of this Atlantean continent, we would find the human form quite different from that of the present. We can go still further back.

Before the Atlantean age, the human being lived in a land which, in the language of today, is called Lemuria. This continent also perished through great changes on our earth. It occupied approximately the region which now lies between southern Asia, Africa, and Australia. When we examine the human forms which lived in Lemuria, as they present themselves to clairvoyant sight, we find them very different from those of present day humanity, and it is not necessary that I describe them to you in detail nor those of the early Atlantean period. Although you have already

had to endure a great deal in the descriptions of Spiritual Science, nevertheless the forms of these ancient Lemurians, fundamentally so different
from the present forms, would appear to you quite improbable. However, we must in a certain respect describe them, although quite superficially if we wish to understand what has happened to the human being
in the course of the earth's evolution.

Let us suppose, for example, something in reality quite impossible, but
we shall assume it for the sake of an understanding. Let us suppose that
with your present senses, which of course you did not at that time possess,
you could look into the latter part of the Lemurian and the first part of
the Atlantean epochs of human evolution, and observe the surface of the
earth in its various parts. If you should expect to be able to find the human
being upon the earth by means of this physical sense perception, you would
be greatly disappointed. At that time he did not exist in a form which
you would be able to see with your present physical senses. It would appear to you as though certain regions of our earth's surface, already re-
sembling islands, protruded out of the rest of the still fluidic earth, which
was either surrounded by sea-water or enveloped in vapour. But those
regions which thus protruded like islands were not yet dry land like our
present solid earth, but soft earth masses in the midst of which fiery
forces played. These island regions were continually being thrown up
and then again submerged by the volcanic forces of that time. In short,
there was still in the earth an element active in fire; all was still actively
in a state of flux, continually changing. In certain regions which already
existed, and which had been cooled to a certain degree, you would find
precursors of our present animal world. Here and there you would have
observed grotesque shapes; you would have found strange forms, forerunners of our reptiles and amphibians. However, you would have been
able to see nothing of the human being, because at that time he did not
possess a physical body dense and solid enough to be seen. You would
have had to seek him elsewhere, as it were, in the masses of water and
vapour. It would be, perhaps, as though you were to swim out to sea
at the present time and could see there not much more of certain lower
animals than a soft, slimy mass. You would then find the human physical
form of that time embedded in the regions of aqueous vapour. The further back we go, the more attenuated and like his vapoury, watery envir-

onment do we find the human form of that period. Not until the Atlantean period does it begin to condense, and were we able to follow with our eyes the whole of evolution, we should be able to see how, out of the water, this human being becomes condensed, gradually descending upon the surface of the earth. As a matter of fact, it is true that the physical human being set foot upon the ground of our earth's surface relatively late. From this region of water and air, he gradually descended, crystallizing out of it. We have now obtained a sketchy picture of a human being who is not distinguishable from his environment, who consists of the same element in which he lives. When we follow very far back in the evolution of the earth, we find that this human body becomes more and more tenuous.

Now let us go back to the very beginning of our present earthly planet. We know that it arose out of the ancient Moon. This ancient Moon we have called the "Cosmos of Wisdom." At a certain stage of its evolution, this ancient Moon did not contain what we would call solid earth, and we must understand very clearly that the physical conditions were quite different on the embodiment of our planet which just preceded our present Earth. If you follow back as far as the ancient Saturn condition, you must not imagine that it would appear as our earth now appears, that you would find rocks upon which you could walk, and trees which you could climb. None of all this existed at that time. If you had approached ancient Saturn during the middle period of its evolution from far out in cosmic space, you would not, perhaps, have seen any special cosmic body moving about, but you would have been able to detect something very strange, namely, that you had come into a region where you felt as though you had crept into an oven. The only reality of this Saturn state was that it possessed a different degree of warmth from its environment. In no other way could it have been perceived. Occultism does not, like the present ordinary physics, distinguish three conditions of matter only, but it discerns still others. The physicist declares that at present there are solid, fluidic and gaseous bodies. Saturn, however, was not yet even gaseous. Our gaseous state is much denser than the densest state on Saturn. In occultism, we distinguish also the state of warmth which is not simply a state of matter in vibration, but a fourth substantial state. Saturn consisted only of this warmth and if we proceed from Saturn to the Sun, we experience a condensation of that ancient fiery planet. The Sun is the first gaseous embodiment of our planet; it is the first gaseous or airy body. The ancient Moon-state then condenses still further; it is a fluid body which only later, when the sun departs from it, assumes a more dense condition. The actual middle condition, however, while it is still united with the sun, is the fluidic state. All that we today call mineral earth, the mineral, rocks, surface soil, all this did not exist on the ancient Moon. This appeared for the first time upon our Earth, crystallizing itself out of it.

When the Earth commenced its evolution, it began by first repeating once more all the various earlier conditions. Every substance and every being in the cosmos always repeats earlier conditions at the beginning of any new stage of evolution. Thus our Earth passed quickly through the Saturn, Sun and Moon states. When it was passing through the Moon evolution, it consisted of water, mixed with vapour—not like our present water, but a watery, that is to say, a fluidic condition of substance. The fluid state was its densest condition. This watery sphere which swam about in cosmic space was not like the water of the present, but water mixed with vapour, in other words, something gaseous and something fluidic permeating each other, and within this we find the human being. He could exist in this watery sphere, because no solid substance had yet been precipitated. Of the present human being, only his ego and his astral body were present. This ego and astral body did not yet feel themselves as separate entities, but as though embedded within the body of divine spiritual beings. They did not yet feel themselves severed from a being whose body is the water-vapour earth. Then within these ego-endowed astral bodies, enclosures were formed, very tenuous, fine human germs. This is shown in the first diagram.

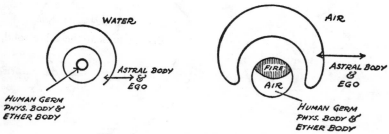

Hyperborean and Lemurian Periods

The upper part of the diagram is intended to represent the astral body and ego which, insensible to outer perception, were embedded in the water-earth sphere; these draw from themselves the first germ of the physical body which together with the ether body was in a very rarefied condition. This then took form out of this watery earth-water sphere. If you were to follow this clairvoyantly, you would see the first germ of the physical and ether bodies surrounded by the astral body and ego as shown in the first figure. That part of you—namely, your physical and ether bodies—which at present lies in bed when you sleep, formed in its very first beginnings in this Earth-state the first human germ still wholly enveloped by the astral body and the ego. The watery vapour mass then densified, and the astral body with the ego gave the impulse to this first human germ to become a part of this primal water-earth. (We cannot now follow further the evolution of the animals and plants.) The next thing that occurred was the condensation of the water, and, in a certain sense, air and water appeared. No longer were vapour and water mixed together, but water and air were separated from one another. As a result, the human corporeality—physical and ether bodies—again became somewhat more densified and because the air had separated from the water, it became airy and took into itself the fiery element. Thus what was formerly watery now became aeriform. The physical ether human germ now consisted of air permeated by fire; the astral body and ego enveloped it and all this moved about in what remained of the water, fluctuating back and forth alternately in water and air.

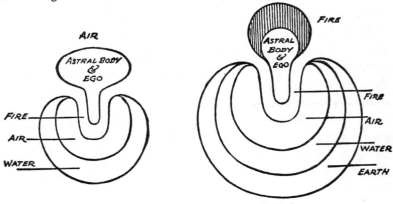

Atlantean and Post-Atlantean Periods

We thus have before us the human being of that time, whose incipient state has reached even the density of air and has been made incalescent by fire. This has become the same human being who lies sleeping in bed today. To each of these human fire-beings belong an astral body and an ego, but they are completely embedded within the bosom of the Godhead, that is, they do not yet feel themselves individualized.

You must meditate deeply upon these things, for these conditions are so different from the present conditions of the earth, they seem shocking and unbelievable. Now you will ask:—What is the fire element which you have indicated there in the air? The fire which human beings possessed at that time still exists within you. It is the fire that pulses through your blood, it is the heat of the blood. What is left over from the ancient air also lives on within your organism. When you inhale and exhale, you have air within your otherwise solid body which flows in and out of it. When you inhale deeply, the air is then taken up into the blood and this is the reason for the warm air-breath. Imagine this air permeating the whole body, penetrating into all its parts. Now, think away all that is solid and fluid and picture only the form that remains, the form of a human being who has just inhaled; that means that he has driven the oxygen into the outermost parts of the body. A form remains which is very similar to the human, but which, however, consists only of air. The air which streams through the human being takes on the exact form of the body. A kind of shadow body remains consisting of air permeated with warmth. That is the kind of human being you were at that time; you did not then have the form which you now possess, but the physical and ether bodies were enveloped by the astral body invested with the ego. This condition continued on into the Atlantean period. Those who yield to the illusion that in the earliest epochs of Atlantis men walked about as they do today, are quite in error. The human creature first descended out of the airy sphere into the denser region of matter. There were at that time upon the earth only the animals who could not hold back their incarnation in physical form, thus they remained at the animal stage, since the earth was not yet mature enough to yield up its substance for the physical human form. Therefore the animals remained in lower forms because they could not hold back their descent into matter.

The next thing that occurred was the division of the human being, in respect of his physical body, into airy, warmth and fluid parts. This means, in an occult sense, that he became a water-man. You may say that the human being was previously already a water-man. But that would not be quite correct. Previously the earth was a watery sphere, and within it—although only in a spiritual state—were astral body and ego. They swam about in the water as spiritual beings; they were not yet individualized. Now we have for the first time reached the point where we could have found the physical human body contained within this water, but in a sort of jelly fish formation. If you had swum out into this primeval sea, you would have found in it, condensed out of the water, forms which would have been transparent to you. This is the way these human beings appeared in the beginning. First they had a water body and at the same time their astral body and ego continued to remain deeply embedded in the divine, spiritual beings. At that time, when the human being possessed this watery body the apportioning of his states of consciousness was very different from what it became later on. The separation into unconscious night and conscious day did not exist as it does now, but then, when the human being was still embedded in the beings of the divine-spiritual world, he had a dreamy astral consciousness. When, during the day, he dipped down into his fluidic, physical body, this was night to him and when he was again out of his physical body, he beheld the dazzling, astral light. When he plunged into the physical body in the morning, there all was dull and dreary and a sort of unconscious state began. Gradually, however, the present physical organs were formed in his physical body and with these he gradually learned to see. Day consciousness became brighter and brighter, and he was thereby cut off from the divine matrix. It was only toward the middle of the Atlantean period that this human creature was dense enough to become flesh and bone. After the cartilage had solidified, the bones then gradually appeared. At the same time the earth also became more solid and the human being then descended upon the surface of the earth. Thus that consciousness which he had possessed in the divine-spiritual world gradually disappeared, and he became more and more an observer of the outer world, preparing himself thereby to become a true earth dweller. In the last third of the Atlantean period, the human form became more and more like the present one.

Thus literally and truly the human being descended from spheres which we must designate water-vapour, water-air spheres. As long as he remained in the water-air sphere, his consciousness possessed the faculty of a clear astral perception, because whenever he was outside of the physical body he was above in the presence of the gods, but by virtue of the densification of the physical body, he cut himself off, as it were, from the divine substance. Like something that had acquired a shell, he slowly severed himself from his earlier connections, when he ceased to be watery and gaseous. As long as he was fluidic and airy in form, he remained above with the gods. He was not able to develop his ego, for he had not yet released himself from the divine consciousness. Because he descended into physical matter, his astral consciousness became ever more darkened. If we wish to characterize the significance of this evolutionary process, we may say that formerly, when the human being was still living with the gods, his physical and ether bodies were fluidic and gaseous in form, and were only gradually, simultaneously with the solidification of the earth, condensed to their present material form. That is the descent, but just as he has made this descent, so will he also ascend again. After he has had the experiences that are to be had in solid substance, he will again mount into those regions where his physical body will be fluidic and gaseous. He must bear within him the consciousness that if he wishes to unite himself again consciously with the gods, his true existence will be in those regions from which he has sprung. He has become condensed out of water and air and he will again become diffused into them. He can only spiritually anticipate this condition today by gaining within his inner nature a consciousness of the future state of his physical body. Only by becoming conscious of it today, however, will he gain the power to do so. When we have acquired this consciousness, our earthly goal will have been reached, our earthly mission attained. What does that mean? It means that human beings were at one time born, not of flesh and earth, but of air and water and that they must later be truly re-born in the Spirit, of air and water.

In the linguistic usage of those epochs in which the Gospels were written, (which we should also study), "Water" was called water; but "Pneuma," which is now used for "Spirit," was then called "Air." It had at one time exactly that meaning. The word "Pneuma" should be translated "Air" or "Vapour," otherwise a misunderstanding arises. Thus we should interpret the words in the conversation with Nicodemus in the following manner: "Verily, verily, I say unto thee, except a man be born of water and air he cannot enter into the Kingdom of Heaven."

The Christ is pointing to a future condition into which the human being will develop, therefore in this conversation we have before us a deep mystery of our evolution. We have only to understand the words correctly and employ them in the manner Anthroposophy can teach us. In the common language of every day, we still have remains of this former usage, when volatile substances are spoken of as spirit. Originally the word "Pneuma" meant air. You can see that it is very important for words to be understood in a very accurate and exact sense and to be carefully weighed. Then out of this very literal meaning arises the most wonderful spiritual interpretation.

Now let us try for a little while to direct our spiritual glance toward another fact of evolution. Let us once more look back to the time when the human astral body with the ego was immersed in the matrix of a common divine astral substance. As you follow this evolutionary course, you find that development took place in such a way that it is possible to describe it schematically. In the beginning, your whole astral being was embedded in the common astral substance and through the processes which we have just described, the physical and etheric enclosed it like surrounding shells. Thus individual human beings became separated from the general astral substance as detached parts. It was as though you had a fluid substance here before you and were dipping out parts of it. The detachment of the individual human consciousness from the divine consciousness runs parallel with the formation of the physical body. Thus we may say that the further we progress, the more we see how the separate individual human beings enclosed in the shell of the physical body, develop themselves as parts which are severed from the common astrality. It is true, the human being had to pay for this becoming independent by the darkening of his astral consciousness. Therefore he looked out from the sheath of his physical body and beheld the physical plane. The ancient clairvoyant consciousness, however, gradually disappeared.

Thus we see coming into existence the human inner being, an independent individual human inner being which is the bearer of the ego. When you observe the sleeping human being of the present, you have before you in the physical and ether bodies, which have remained behind in bed, what these sheaths, formed during the course of the ages, have produced through condensation. What had previously separated from the common astral substance returns to it each night in order to receive strength from it. Of course it does not enter so deeply into this divine substance as it did at that time, otherwise it would be clairvoyant. It retains its independence. This, then, is the independent individuality that came into existence in the course of evolution.

It may be asked, to what is this independent individual human being indebted for its very existence, this inner being that seeks its strength outside the physical and ether bodies? It is indebted to the physical and ether human bodies which were gradually formed in the course of evolution. They gave birth to that which dipped down into the physical senses and looked out into the physical world during the day, but which at night sank down into a state of unconsciousness, because it had severed itself from that condition in which it previously existed. In occult language, the part remaining in bed is called the real earth-man. That was "man." And that part in which the ego remained day and night, that part born out of the physical and ether bodies was called the "child of man" or the "son of man." The "son of man" is the ego and astral body, born out of the physical and ether bodies in the course of earthly evolution. The technical expression for this is the "son of man."

Then comes the question, for what purpose did Christ Jesus come to earth; what was imparted to the earth through His Impulse? The "son of man" who had severed himself from existence in the bosom of the Godhead and had broken away from his earlier connections, and in place of which developed a physical consciousness will come again to a consciousness of the spirit through the force of the Christ Who appeared upon the earth. He will not only perceive in his physical environment with physical senses, but by means of the force of his own inner being of which he is now unconscious, a consciousness of his divine existence will flash up within him. Through the force of the Christ Who came upon the earth, the son of man will again be raised to his divine estate. Previously, after the manner of the ancient Mystery initiation, only chosen individuals could perceive the divine-spiritual world. In ancient times there was a technical expression for this. Those who could look into the divine-spiritual world and could become witnesses of it were called "serpents." Those men of ancient times who were initiated into the Mysteries in this way were "serpents." The "serpents" were the forerunners of the deed of Christ Jesus. Moses showed his mission by lifting up before his people the symbol of the elevation of those who could perceive in the spiritual worlds; he lifted up the serpent. What these chosen few had then become, now every "son of man" could attain through the force of the Christ present upon the earth. This the Christ expresses in his further conversation with Nicodemus when He says:—"Just as once upon a time Moses lifted up the serpent, even so will the son of man be lifted up." Throughout, Christ Jesus made use of the technical expressions of that age. First the literal sense of the expressions must be discovered, then the true meaning can be understood; this is also identical with the Anthroposophical teaching. Therefore, in ancient times only a prophecy of the "I AM" teaching could gain a footing. Only on the outer authority of the initiated could the people hear something of the power of the "I AM" which should be enkindled in every "son of man." But we are quite sufficiently informed about this.

We have seen what the "I AM" signifies in the Gospel of St. John and can ask whether this "I AM" in the course of time has been imparted to humanity. Has it been gradually proclaimed? Did the Old Testament prophetically point to and prepare for what was brought to mankind as an impulse through the descent of the incarnated "I AM"?

Please remember that all that occurs in the course of the ages has been slowly and gradually prepared before-hand. Like the child in the mother's womb, all that was brought by Jesus-Christ had been slowly matured in the followers of the Old Testament through the ancient Mysteries. On the other hand what had been prepared in the followers of the Old Testament among the ancient Jewish peoples had grown to maturity among the ancient Egyptians. Among them were highly developed initiates who knew what was to come upon the earth. We shall now learn how the Egyptians, who were the third sub-race of the post-Atlantean root-race, developed by degrees the complete impulse of the "I AM," and how they furnished, like the mother's womb, the outer structure for this "I AM," but did not go far enough to give birth to the Christ Principle. Then we shall learn how at last the ancient Hebrew peoples separated from them.

Moses is represented to us as one chosen from among the people of Egypt to become the prophet of God, of the incarnated "I AM." He prophesied the coming of the "I AM" to those who could understand something of It. He announced that for the words, "I and Father Abraham are one," will be substituted these other words, "I and the Father are one," which means, I and the spiritual foundation of the World are directly one. The followers of the Old Testament looked up to the folk group-soul in its plurality and in this group-soul, each individual felt sheltered as though within the Divine. Through Moses, an initiate of the old order, it was prophesied that the Christ would come; in other words, that there is a divine principle which is higher than the blood-principle flowing down through the generations. It is true, God has been active in the blood since the time of Abraham, but this blood-father is only the outer manifestation of the spiritual Father.

Moses said unto God, Who am I that I should go unto Pharaoh, and that I should bring forth the children of Israel out of Egypt?

He said, I will be with thee: and this shall be a sign that I have sent thee: When thou hast brought forth my people out of Egypt, ye shall serve God upon this mountain.

And Moses said unto God: Behold, when I come unto the children of Israel, and shall say unto them: The God of your fathers hath sent me unto you, and they say unto me: What is his name? What shall I say unto them?

He had to announce prophetically a more exalted God, Who exists within the God of Father Abraham, but Who is at the same time a higher Principle. What is His name?

And God said unto Moses, I am the "I AM"!

Here is foretold the profound truth about the Word which later appeared incarnate in Christ-Jesus.

And he said: Thus shalt thou say unto the children of Israel: the "I AM" hath taught it to me.

This is the literal wording. In other words, this means that the "name," that name which is the basis of the blood-name, is the "I AM"—and this "I AM" appears incarnate in the Christ of the Gospel of St. John.

And God said further unto Moses, Thus thou shalt say unto the children of Israel, the Lord, God of your fathers, the God of Abraham, the God of Isaac, the God of Jacob hath sent me unto you.

What has been seen only externally streaming through the blood, is in its deeper meaning, the "I AM."

Thus was proclaimed what was later to enter the world through Christ-Jesus. We hear the name of the Logos, we hear Him at that time calling to Moses, "I am the I AM!" The Logos proclaims His name, that part of Himself which can be comprehended through the understanding, through the intellect. What is here proclaimed appears in the flesh as the Logos, is incarnated in Christ-Jesus.

Now let us consider the external sign of the flowing down of the Logos into the Israelitish people, as far as this can be grasped abstractly in thought. This outer sign is the "Manna" of the Wilderness. The word "Manna" is, in fact, (those who understand Spiritual Science know this) the same as "Manas" [1], the "Spirit-Self." Thus there streams into that people which has by degrees acquired an I-consciousness, the first trace of the Spirit-Self. However that which lives and appears in Manas itself must be called by another name. It is not something that can be simply known, but it is a force which can be taken into oneself. When the Logos simply proclaimed His name, it could be understood and grasped with the intellect. But when the Logos became flesh and appeared among men, then it became a Force-Impulse which is not only a teaching and a concept, but exists in the world as a Force-Impulse in which humanity can participate. He then calls Himself no longer "Manna," but the "Bread of Life," which is the technical expression for Budhi or Life-Spirit.

[1] Note by translator. Dr. Steiner was giving these lectures to Theosophists who were familiar with the oriental terminology. By degrees he dropped this as the students became familiar with his own new occidental terms.

The water transformed by the spirit, which was offered in symbolic form to the Samaritan woman, and the "Bread of Life" are the first heraldings of the influx of Budhi or Life-Spirit into mankind. Tomorrow we shall continue this discussion.

VII

THE MYSTERY OF GOLGOTHA

The whole of the Gospel of St. John culminates in that event in human history which we call the "Mystery of Golgotha." To comprehend this Mystery of Golgotha esoterically predicates also the ability to decipher the deep significance of this Gospel. If we turn our attention to what exists at the very central point of this Mystery and wish to express it in occult terms, we must contemplate the moment of the Crucifixion when the blood flowed from the wounds of the Saviour, and at the same time we must remember something which has often been said in the course of these lectures, that for one who knows the spiritual worlds, all material, substantial, physical objectivity is only the outer expression, the external manifestation of something spiritual. Now let us permit the physical event to arise before our souls: Christ-Jesus upon the Cross, the blood flowing from His wounds. What does this picture, the content of which is a physical event, express for those who are able to understand the Gospel of St. John?

This physical event—the occurrence on Golgotha—is the expression, the manifestation of a spiritual event which stands at the central point of all earthly happenings. Anyone interpreting these words according to the present materialistic world concept will not be able to make much out of them, for he will not be able to imagine that at that time something occurred in this unique Event of Golgotha which differs from some other like event, or from one perhaps physically similar. There is a very great difference between all the earthly occurrences which preceded this Event of Golgotha and those that succeed it.

If we wish to picture this in the soul in all its detail, we must say that not only has the individual human being, or for that matter any other individual creature, a physical, ether and astral body as we have described it from many aspects in the foregoing lectures, but that cosmic bodies likewise do not consist only of physical substance as they appear to the astronomer and to other physical researchers. A cosmic body has also an ether and an astral body. Our earth has its ether and astral vehicles. If our earth did not possess its own ether body, it would not be able to harbour the plants; if it did not possess its own individual astral body, it would not be able to shelter the animals. If we wish to visualize the earth's ether body, we must imagine its central point exactly at the center of the earth where the physical earth body also has its central point. This entire physical earth body is embedded in its own ether body and these two are again embedded in an astral body. If someone had observed clairvoyantly the astral body of the earth during the course of the earth's evolution, during the course of long epochs of time, he would have seen that, as a matter of fact, this astral body and ether body of the earth have not always remained the same, that they have changed. In order to represent the matter quite pictorially, let us in spirit transplant ourselves outside beyond the earth to some other star, and let us imagine a person with clairvoyant vision looking down upon the earth from this star. He would not only see the earth suspended there as a physical planet, but he would see an aura about it, he would see the earth surrounded by an aura of light, for he would be perceiving the earth's ether and astral bodies. If this clairvoyant person were to remain a long time on this distant star, long enough to have observed the pre-Christian periods of the earth pass by and the Event of Golgotha approaching, the following spectacle would have presented itself to him. Before the Event of Golgotha the aura of the earth, the astral and ether bodies offered a certain aspect of colour and form, but following a particular, definite moment of time, he would have seen the colour of the entire aura changing. What was this particular moment of time? It was the very moment when the blood flowed from the wounds of Christ-Jesus upon Golgotha. All spiritual earthly relationships, as such, changed from this moment.

It has been previously stated that what is called the Logos is the sum total of the six Elohim who, united with the sun, present the earth with their spiritual gifts, while externally the physical sunlight is falling upon the earth. Therefore the light of the sun appears to us like the outer physical body of the spirit and soul of the Elohim or of the Logos. At the moment of the Event of Golgotha, that force, that impulse which formerly could only stream down upon the earth as light began to unite with the earth itself. And because the Logos began to unite with the earth, the earth's aura became changed.

We shall now consider the Event of Golgotha from still another point of view. We have already reviewed the evolution of the human being and of the earth from various standpoints. We know that our Earth, before it became the Earth, passed through the three embodiments of Saturn, Sun and Moon. Therefore the embodiment just preceding that of our Earth was that of the ancient Moon. When a planet has attained the goal of its evolution, something happens to it similar to what happens to a human being who, in a certain incarnation, has attained his life's goal. The planet passes over into a different invisible existence, a state called a "Pralaya" and then after a time it embodies itself anew. Thus between the previous embodiment of our Earth, the Moon Evolution, and the Earth's present embodiment, there existed an intermediate state Out of a sort of spiritual, self-animated, externally invisible existence, the Earth gleamed forth in its earliest state and out of this state developed those states which we described yesterday. At that time, in that early age when our Earth gleamed forth, it was still united with all that now belongs to our solar system. It was then so large, that it reached to the furthest planets of this solar system. All was unity, for only later individual planets became segregated. The present earth up to a certain point of time was united with our present sun and moon. Thus we see there was a time when sun, moon and earth were a single body. It was as though you were to take the present moon and sun and stir them together with the earth and thus make one large cosmic body. This was our Earth once upon a time when your astral body and your ego were floating about in a vapour-like form. Even earlier than this the sun, moon and earth were joined together. At that time the forces which are now in the sun—the spiritual and physical forces—were bound up with the earth. Then came a time when the sun separated from the earth; but not only did the physical sun with its physical light which can be seen with physical eyes depart, but with it all its spiritual and soul beings at whose head stood the Elohim, the real Spirits of Light, the denizens of the sun. What was left, was a mixture of the present moon and earth. Then for a time the earth, though separated from the sun, was still united with the moon. It was not until the Lemurian period that the moon separated from the earth, when, as a result, there arose that relationship between these three bodies, sun, moon and earth, that exists today. This relationship had to occur. The Elohim had to act from without. It was necessary for one of them to become Lord of the moon and from there reflect the powerful force of the other Elohim. We live at present upon our earth as though dwelling upon an island in cosmic space which has separated from the sun and moon. But the time will come when our earth will once more unite with the sun and again form one body with it. Then human beings will be so spiritualized that they will again be able to bear the stronger forces of the sun, able to receive them and unite them with themselves. They, together with the Elohim, will then occupy the same field of action.

You will ask, what is the force that will bring this about? Had the Event of Golgotha not occurred, the earth and the sun would never be able to reunite. For through the Event of Golgotha, which bound the force of the Elohim in the sun to the earth—in other words the force of the Logos—the impulse was given which will again eventually impel one Logos-force toward the other, and finally once more unite them—sun and earth—in one body. Since the Event of Golgotha, the earth, spiritually observed, is possessed of the force to draw the sun again into a unity with it. Therefore it can be said that through this great Event, the force of the Logos, which formerly radiated down upon the earth from without, was now taken up into its spiritual being. The question may be asked, what existed previously within the body of the earth? It was that force which streamed down upon it from the sun. But since that time, what exists there within the earth? The Logos itself which through Golgotha has become the spirit of the earth.

As truly as your soul and spirit dwell within your physical body, do also the soul and spirit of the earth dwell within the body of the earth—that earthly body which consists of stones, plants and animals and upon which you tread. This soul and spirit, this earth spirit is the Christ. Christ is the spirit of the earth. When the Christ spoke to His most trusted disciples on an occasion which can be numbered among the most intimate of such occasions, what did He say to them? With what mystery had He occasion to entrust them? He was able to say to them: "It is as though you can gaze into your own soul from your physical body. Your soul is within. It is the same when you observe the whole earth-sphere. That spirit which for a time now stands here before you in the flesh is also the spirit of the earth and will always continue as such." He had occasion to point to the earth as to His real body and ask: "When you behold the cornfield and then eat the bread that nourishes you, what in reality is this bread which you are eating? You are eating My body. And when you drink of the plant sap, it is like the blood in your own body; it is the blood of the earth—My Blood!"—These were the very words that Christ-Jesus spoke to His most intimate disciples and we must take them very literally. Then when He called them together and expounded to them symbolically what we shall call the Christian Initiation, He uttered those extraordinary words which we find in the 18th verse of the 13th Chapter of the Gospel of St. John, where He announced that one among them would betray Him:

"He who eats My bread treads me under foot."

These words must be taken literally. Men eat the bread of the earth and tread upon the earth with their feet. If the earth is the body of the Earth-Spirit, that is, of the Christ, then men tread with their feet the earth's body, the body whose bread they eat. An immense deepening of the idea of the Last Supper as presented in the Gospel of St. John is granted us, when we learn about the Christ, the Earth-Spirit, and about the bread which is taken from the body of the earth. Christ points to the earth and says: "This is My body!" Just as the muscular human flesh belongs to the human soul, so does bread belong to the body of the earth, that is to the body of the Christ. And the sap that flows through the plants, which pulsates through the vine stalk, is like the blood pulsating through the human body. Pointing to this, the Christ says: "This is my blood!" That this truthful explanation of the Last Supper can cause some of the sanctity to be lost which has always been associated with it can only be imagined by someone possessing no understanding of it or who has neither desire nor capacity for such an understanding. But anyone who wishes to understand will acknowledge that this does not cause it to lose in holiness, but that through it the whole of the earth-planet becomes sanctified. What powerful feelings can be engendered in our souls, if we can behold in the Last Supper the greatest mystery of the earth, the connection between the Event of Golgotha and the entire evolution of the earth; if we can learn to feel that in the Last Supper the flowing of the blood from the wounds of the Saviour had not only a human, but a cosmic significance, that is, it gave to the earth the force to carry forward its evolution.

Anyone who understands the profound meaning of the Gospel of St. John will feel not only united through his physical body with the physical body of the earth, but as a psycho-spiritual being will feel united with the psycho-spiritual being of the earth which is the Christ Himself, and then he will feel how the Christ, as the Spirit of the Earth, flows through his body. When we have this experience, we are able to ask: what illuminated the writer of the Gospel of St. John at that moment when he was able to behold the profound mysteries which have to do with Christ-Jesus? He beheld the forces, the impulses which are present in Christ-Jesus, and he perceived how these impulses must be active in mankind, if only mankind will receive them.

In order to understand this quite clearly, we must once more bring before our souls the way in which human evolution actually takes place. The human being consists of physical, ether and astral bodies and an ego. How does this evolution occur? By the ego gradually working through the other three members, purifying and strengthening them. The ego is called upon gradually to purify the astral body, to cleanse it and to raise it to a higher level. When the entire astral body has been purified and strengthened by the special forces of the ego, it becomes Manas or Spirit-Self. When the ether or life-body has been thoroughly worked over and strengthened by the force of the ego, it becomes Budhi, or Life-Spirit. When the physical body has been fully overcome and conquered by the ego, it becomes Atman or Spirit-Man. Then will the human being have reached the goal which above all lies in store for him. That, however, will be attained only in the far distant future. Moreover, we wish it to be quite clear that the ego acts in full consciousness in what has just been described; namely, that the human being consisting of the four members—physical, ether and astral bodies and ego—works by means of the ego upon the other three members, transforming them into Spirit-Self, Life-Spirit and Spirit-Man. For the most part this is not yet the case with present humanity which, as a matter of fact, is just beginning, fully conscious, to work a little of Manas into its astral body. The human being is doing this now. Through the help of higher beings he has already, al-though unconsciously, worked upon his three lower members during this

Earth evolution. In ancient times he unconsciously worked over the astral body, and this then became permeated by the Sentient Soul. The ego unconsciously worked into the ether body and this unconsciously re-formed ether body is what you will find described in regular sequence in my book *Theosophy* as the Intellectual Soul, and that part of the physical body, unconsciously worked upon by the ego, you will find described there as the Consciousness Soul. The Consciousness Soul only came into being toward the end of the Atlantean period when the ether body—previously outside the physical body in the head region—gradually drew wholly within it. Through this the human being learned to utter the word "I." Thus variously-membered, he gradually passed over into the post-Atlantean period. It is the task of our age to work Manas or Spirit-Self by degrees into what had previously been received unconsciously. The human being must, as it were, develop Manas within himself by means of all the forces he has acquired by virtue of possessing a physical, an ether and an astral body, a sentient, an intellectual and a consciousness soul; by means of all the forces which these various members can give him, he must develop Manas and also, although in a very small degree, the germ of a Life-Spirit or Budhi. Therefore our post-Atlantean age has the important task of helping the human being to develop *consciously* these higher members of his being (Manas or Spirit-Self, Budhi or Life-Spirit and Atman or Spirit-Man) in the distant future when he will at last have reached his goal. He must from now on, by degrees, develop within himself the force to evolve his higher members out of his lower.

Let us now ask: what has been the condition of the human being that has kept him from already developing these higher members, and what will be the difference in the future? How will the humanity of the future differ from that of the present?

When at last the whole of the higher man has been developed, the entire astral body will be so completely purified that it will simultaneously become Manas or Spirit-Self; the ether body so thoroughly purged that it will simultaneously become Life-Spirit or Budhi, and the physical body will be so greatly metamorphosed that it will, at the same time, be as actually a Spirit-Man, Atman, as it is now a physical body. The greatest force will be needed to conquer this lowest body, hence the conquest and transformation of the physical means the greatest victory for the human being. When mankind has fully perfected the physical body, this physical man will then become Spirit-Man or Atman. All this is at present only in germ within the human being, but a time will come when it will live in him in its fulness. And by lifting his gaze to the Christ Personality, to the Christ Impulse, by energizing and strengthening himself through this Christ Impulse, he draws into himself the force that can accomplish this transformation.

Since humanity of the present has not yet perfected this metamorphosis, what is the result? Spiritual Science makes this very clear. Because this katharsis of the astral body has not yet been accomplished, that is, the astral body has not yet transformed itself into Spirit-Self, selfishness or egotism is possible. Because the ether body has not yet been strengthened by the ego, lying and error are possible; and because the physical body has not yet been fortified by the ego, sickness and death are possible. In a once fully developed Spirit-Self, there will be no more selfishness; no sickness and death, but just health and salvation in the fully developed Spirit-Man, that is, in the fully evolved physical body. What does it mean for the human being to take the Christ into himself? It means that he has learned to understand the forces that are in the Christ, which if taken into himself make it possible for him to become master even of his physical body.

Imagine for example that someone could receive the Christ Impulse fully into himself, that it could completely pass over upon him. The Christ Himself might stand directly in the presence of this person and the Christ Impulse be transmitted to him. What does that signify? If the person were blind, he would yet be able to see by means of the direct influence of this Christ Impulse, for the final goal of evolution is the conquest of the forces of sickness and death. When the writer of the Gospel of St. John speaks of the healing of the man born blind, he is then speaking out of the depths of the Mysteries, he is demonstrating, by means of an example, that the force of the Christ is a healing force when it appears in full power. It may be asked: Where is this force? It is in the body of the Christ, in the earth! But this earth must, in truth, be fully permeated by the being of the Christ Spirit or of the Logos. Let us see if the writer of the Gospel recounts the story with this meaning. How does he relate it?

Standing there is the blind man. The Christ takes some earth, insalivates it and lays it upon the blind man's eyes. He lays His body, the earth, permeated with His spirit upon the blind man. In this description, the writer of the Gospel indicates a mystery which he very well understands. Now laying aside all prejudice, let us talk a little more in detail of this sign—one of the greatest performed by the Christ—in order that we may learn to know more exactly the nature of such a thing and not be disturbed because our very clever contemporaries will consider what has just been said to be sheer madness or folly! There are, however, in the world great and mighty mysteries which mankind is not yet entitled to know. Human beings of the present day, even though they may be sufficiently developed, are not yet strong enough to go through the great Mysteries. They can know of them, they can understand them when they are able to experience them spiritually; but our present humanity, so deeply immersed in matter, is not yet capable of converting them into their physical expression.

All life is, in fact, made up of antitheses and extremes. Life and death are just such extremes. For the thought and feelings of the occultist, there is something very extraordinary in seeing, for example, a corpse and a living human being side by side. When we have a living, waking human being before us, we know that a soul and spirit dwell within him. But as far as consciousness is concerned, this soul and spirit are, as it were, cut off from any connection with the spiritual world; they cannot look into it. If we have a corpse before us, we have the feeling that the spirit and soul which once belonged to it are passing over into the spiritual worlds where consciousness, or the light of those worlds is flashing up within them. Thus the corpse becomes a symbol of what is taking place in the spiritual world. But in the physical world also, there are reflections of what is happening in the spiritual world, but they are of an extraordinary character. When a human being descends again into physical birth, his bodily part must be reconstructed; material substance must, so to say, rush together in order that a body be created for him. For the clairvoyant, this rushing together of physical substance represents the death of consciousness in the spirit world. There it dies—here it becomes alive. In the rushing together of substance to form a physical human body can be seen, in a certain sense, the dying of a spiritual consciousness; while on the other hand, at the moment of decomposition or of the burning of the physical body, when the parts disintegrate and dissolve, the opposite actually becomes manifest in the spiritual world, that is, the awakening of a spiritual consciousness occurs. Physical dissolution is spiritual birth. Therefore all processes of decay and dissolution mean something more than just decay and dissolution to the occultist. A church-yard, spiritually observed, where physical bodies are in the process of dis-solution, is the scene of remarkable processes, the continuous flashing up and glistening of spiritual birth; (I am now speaking of what is taking place spiritually in the churchyard itself apart from the human beings there).

Let us imagine for example that a person were to give himself up physically to a certain training—naturally no one would recommend this, for the present physical body could not possibly endure it—to a schooling in which he would train his body to breathe in putrified air for a certain prescribed length of time with the conscious intent of taking in the spiritual processes which have just been described. If he does this in the proper way, then in his following incarnations—it cannot be done in one —he can be incarnated with that force which offers restorative and health-giving impulses. Breathing putrid air belongs to a schooling which grad-ually gives strength to the spittle, when mixed with the ordinary earth, to become the healing substance which the Christ rubbed upon the eyes of the blind man. This mystery through which a person consumes, eats or inhales death, by which he acquires the power to heal, is the mystery to which the writer of the Gospel refers when he describes such signs as the healing of the man born blind. Instead of declaring without cessation that such and such a thing should be interpreted to mean thus and so, it would be much better were people to learn that such a thing as is described in the healing of the blind man is literally true, that it exists, and that it is possible to have respect for such a personality as the writer of the Gospel and be able to say: "There was such a person who was thoroughly initiated into this mystery about which we must try to acquire an understanding."

It was, moreover, necessary to call attention beforehand to the fact that we are here in an anthroposophical group in which many prejudices have been eliminated, thus making it possible to speak of such real mys-teries as the insalivation of the earth's soil for healing purposes, and to say that such an incident has a literal significance.

However, let us now try to comprehend how, by knowing these facts, we unite with the idea that occupies us today namely, that the Christ is the Spirit of the earth and that the earth is His Body. We have seen the Christ spiritualizing the etheric element in one instance and have seen Him giving up something of Himself in order to perform the miracle we are considering. Now let us consider something else. Besides what has been said today, let us take what the Christ Himself said: "The most profound mystery of My being is the I AM, and the true and eternal might of the I AM or of the Ego which has the force to permeate other bodies must flow into human beings. It dwells within the Earth Spirit." Let us hold this clearly in mind and take very earnestly, quite seriously, the fact that, because the Christ wishes to bestow the true ego upon every human soul, He will awaken the God in it and gradually enkindle the Spirit of the Lord and King in everyone. What does this signify? We have here nothing more nor less than the fact that the Christ brings to expression, in the highest sense, the idea of Karma, the karmic law. For when anyone fully understands the idea of Karma, he will understand it in this Christian sense. It means that no man should set himself up as a judge of the inner soul of another human being. Unless the idea of Karma has been understood in this way, it has not been grasped in its deepest significance. When one man judges another, the one is always placing the other under the compulsion of his own ego. However, if a person really believes in the "I AM" in the Christian sense, he will not judge. He will say: "I know that Karma is the great adjuster. Whatever you may have done, I do not judge it!"

Let us suppose that a transgressor is brought before a person who really understands the Christ-Word. What will be his attitude toward the transgressor? Let us suppose that all those who would like to be Christians were to accuse him of a terrible sin. The real Christian would say to them: "Whether what you maintain has been done by him or not, makes no difference, the I AM must be respected; it must be left to Karma, to the great law which is the law of the Christ-Spirit Himself. Karma is fulfilled in the course of earthly evolution. We can leave it to this earthly evolution to determine what *punishment* Karma shall inflict upon a human being." He would perhaps turn to the earth and say to the accusers:—"Pay heed to yourselves, it is the duty of the earth to inflict the punishment. Let us inscribe it then upon the earth where it has, moreover, been registered as Karma."

Jesus went up to the Mount of Olives.

And early in the morning He came again into the temple and all the people came unto Him and He sat down and taught them.

And the scribes and Pharisees brought unto Him a woman taken in adultery; and they placed her in their midst.

They said unto Him, Master, this woman was taken in adultery in the very act. Now Moses in the law commanded us that such should be stoned; but what sayest Thou?

This they said, tempting Him, that they might accuse Him. But Jesus stooped down and with His finger wrote on the ground.

So when they continued asking Him, He lifted Himself up and said unto them, He that is without sin among you, let him first cast a stone at her.

And again He stooped down and wrote on the ground.

But when they heard this, being convicted by their own conscience, they went out one by one, beginning at the eldest even unto the last: and Jesus was left alone, and the woman standing in the midst.

When Jesus had lifted Himself up and saw none but the woman, He said unto her, Woman, where are those thine accusers? Hath no man condemned thee?

This He said in order to turn her thoughts away from all idea of outer judgment and point to an inner Karma.

She said, No man, Lord.

She was left to her Karma. Thus the only thing for her was to think no more about "punishment" which Karma fulfills, but to change her life.

And Jesus said unto her, Neither do I condemn thee: go, and sin no more.

Thus we see that the idea of Karma is bound up with the idea of the Christ in its deepest sense, is connected with the very significance of His Being for the earth. "If you have understood my Being, then you have comprehended also Him whose Being I express and know that the I AM brings compensation." The impulse to independence and an inner completion is what the Christ has given to mankind.

Humanity has not even today attained a very great understanding of true, esoteric Christianity. However, when men learn to understand what is to be found in such a writing as the Gospel of St. John, they will by degrees take into themselves the Impulse present in it. Then in a far distant future, the Christian ideal will be accomplished.

Thus we see that in the post-Atlantean period the first impulse for developing the higher man flows into the earth. Tomorrow we shall become acquainted with the evolution of the human being in his relation to the Christ Impulse here in this post-Atlantean period and then, proceeding further, we shall show what the Christ of the future will be.

VIII

HUMAN EVOLUTION IN ITS RELATION TO THE
CHRIST PRINCIPLE

We have seen that we come closer to the profound meaning of the Gospel of St. John when we seek to approach it from various sides, and yesterday we were able from a certain point of view to indicate one of the most significant mysteries of this Gospel. In order that we may gradually reach a complete understanding of the mystery presented yesterday, it will now be necessary to consider the advent of Christ-Jesus in our post-Atlantean period. We have gathered together the most varied material in order that we might trace the evolution of the human being and within it the Christ Principle. Today we shall try to understand why, just at this point of time in our evolution, the Christ appeared as a human being walking upon the earth and we shall in this way form a connection with what we have already heard in part in the last lectures. Now we shall have to consider especially the evolution of our humanity in the post-Atlantean period.

We have repeatedly stated that at a time very far in the past our forefathers dwelt out there in the west in a region now occupied by the Atlantic Ocean. Our forebears dwelt upon old Atlantis. In the lecture of the day before yesterday we were able to call attention especially to the external bodily appearance of these our Atlantean forefathers. We have seen that the physical body, visible now to the external human sense organs, only slowly and gradually reached the present density of flesh which it now possesses. We said that not until the last part of the Atlantean period did men bear some resemblance to their present form. Even toward the last third of the Atlantean period they were still essentially very different creatures from the men of today, although to the external senses they appeared much the same. We can best make clear what progress the human being has made, if we compare him in his present state with any of the existing higher animals. However highly developed the animal may be, it must now be clear for various reasons how the human being differs essentially from the animal. We find that upon the physical plane or in the physical world, every animal consists of physical body, ether or life body and astral body; that these three parts compose its animal being in the physical world.

You must not imagine that only what is *physical* exists in the physical world. It would be a great mistake if you were to seek all that is etheric or in fact all that is astral only in the supersensible world. It is true you can see only what is physical with the physical senses in the physical world, but that is not because only what is physical exists here. No, the ether and astral bodies of the animals are present in the physical world and the clairvoyantly endowed person can see them. It is only when he wishes to reach the real ego of the animal that he can no longer remain in the physical world; he must then mount into the astral regions. There the group-soul or group-ego of the animals is to be found and the difference between the human being and the animal consists in the ego of the former also being present here below in the physical world. This means that here in the physical world, the human creature consists of a physical, ether and astral body and an ego, although the three higher members, from the ether body upwards, are only perceptible to clairvoyant consciousness. This difference between the human being and the animal is expressed clairvoyantly in a certain way. Let us suppose that a person endowed with clairvoyance is observing a horse and a man. Extending beyond the horse's head, which is lengthened out to a muzzle, he finds an etheric appendage. This etheric head protrudes beyond the physical head of the horse and is magnificently organized; these two do not coincide in the horse. But he finds that in the human being of the present, the etheric head corresponds almost exactly in form and size to the physical. Clairvoyantly observed, the elephant makes an extremely grotesque appearance with its extraordinarily huge etheric head; it is, indeed, etherically a very grotesque animal. In the human beings of the present, the physical and etheric heads coincide and in form and size they are very nearly alike. This, however, has not always been the case. We find it so only in the last third of the Atlantean period. The ancient Atlanteans' etheric head protruded far beyond his physical head, then by degrees these two grew together and it was in the last third of the Atlantean period that the physical and the etheric heads exactly coincided. In the brain, near the eyes, there is a point which coincides with a very definite point in the etheric head. These points were apart in ancient times; the etheric point was outside of the brain. These two important points have drawn together and only when this occurred did the human being learn to say "I" to himself. Then appeared what we yesterday called the "Consciousness Soul." Through the coincidence of the etheric and physical heads, the appearance of the human head changed very greatly, for the head of the ancient Atlantean was still very different in appearance from the head of present human beings. If we wish to understand how the present evolution became possible, we must consider a little the physical conditions in ancient Atlantis.

If you had been able to walk through ancient Atlantis, out there in the west, you would not have been able to experience the conditions of rain, fog, air and sunshine that we have now in our present earth. At that time mists pervaded especially the northern regions, west of Scandinavia. Those human beings who lived in ancient Atlantis, in the region where Ireland now stands and even further to the West, never saw rain and sunshine as separate phenomena as is now the case. They were always immersed in mist and only with the Atlantean Flood did the time come when the fog banks separated from the air and were precipitated into the ocean. You might have searched through the whole of Atlantis and you would not have found that spectacle which is now well known to you all as an extraordinary phenomenon of nature; it would have been impossible to discover a rainbow. That is only possible through a separation of rain and sunshine such as can now exist in the atmosphere. On Atlantis before the Flood, you would have found no rainbow. Only gradually, after the Flood, did this phenomenon appear, that is, it became a physical possibility. If after having received these communications of Spiritual Science, you recall that the memory of the Atlantean Flood is preserved in the various sagas and myths of the Deluge and that after the Deluge, Noah came forth and first saw the rainbow, then you will get some idea of how literally and profoundly true the religious documents are. It is a fact that human beings first saw a rainbow after the Atlantean Flood. These are the experiences which can be had by one who acquaints himself with occultism, and then bit by bit learns to understand how literally the religious documents must be taken. Of course one must first learn to understand the alphabet.

Towards the end of the Atlantean period, the external and internal human conditions proved to be most favorable in a certain region of the earth's surface which was in the vicinity of present Ireland. This region is now covered with water. At that time the conditions there were especially favourable and in this region the most highly gifted of the Atlantean races developed, a race that was especially endowed with the capacity to rise to an independent human self-consciousness. The leader of this people, which in Spiritual Science literature is usually designated the ancient Semites, was a great initiate who sought the most highly developed individuals of this people and migrated with them to the east through Europe as far as Asia into a region occupied now by the present Tibet. Thither migrated a relatively small but spiritually very highly developed fraction of the Atlantean peoples. Toward the end of the Atlantean period, it so happened that gradually the westerly portions of Atlantis disappeared and became covered by the sea. Europe in its present form gradually arose. In Asia, the great Siberian regions were still covered with extensive bodies of water, but, especially in the south of Asia, there were regions of land which had already appeared, differently formed, however. Some of the less advanced of the great mass of people joined with this germinal group which migrated from west to east. Many went with them a long distance, others not so far. But the peopling of ancient Europe came about for the most part through the migrations of great hordes of people out of Atlantis who settled there. Other great groups of people who had been driven from other parts of Atlantis, even some from ancient Lemuria, had come into Asia at a still earlier period and now encountered each other during this migration. Thus peoples variously endowed and of very different spiritual capacities settled in Europe and Asia. The small number who were led by that great spiritual individuality, Manu, settled there in Asia in order to foster the greatest possible spirituality. From there streams of culture flowed out into the various regions of the earth and among the various peoples.

The first cultural stream flowed down into India, and through the impulse given by the spiritual mission of that great individuality, Manu, there developed what we may call the ancient Indian civilization. We are not speaking now of that Indian culture of which we have only echoes in those wonderful books of the Vedas, nor are we speaking of what has been handed down to posterity as tradition. Previous to all that can be known of this external culture, there existed a much more glorious and more ancient culture, that of the ancient Holy Rishis, those great teachers who in the far distant past gave to mankind the first post-Atlantean civilization. Let us transplant ourselves into the souls of the people of this first post-Atlantean cultural stream. This was the first really religious human culture. Those Atlantean cultural periods which preceded this one were not religious cultural epochs in the true sense of the word. Religion is, in fact, a characteristic of the post-Atlantean age. You will ask, why is this the case?

Let us see how Atlanteans lived. Since the etheric head was still outside of the physical head, the ancient hazy clairvoyance was not yet completely lost. Therefore, at night, when the Atlantean was outside of his physical body, he could look into the furthest reaches of the spiritual world. Although during the day—when he dipped down into his physical body—he saw physical things here in the physical world, at night he still saw, to a certain degree, the regions of the spiritual world. Transfer yourselves now for a moment into the middle or first third of the Atlantean period. What was the condition of the human being then? He awakened in the morning and his astral body was drawn into his physical and ether bodies. At that time the objects of the physical world were not yet so sharply and clearly contoured as they are now. When a city is enveloped in fog, and you observe the lanterns in the evening as though surrounded by an aura of color with undefined edges and streams of color, you have in this a picture of how things appeared at that time on Atlantis. The outlines were not clearly defined, but it was like seeing the lanterns in the mist. Hence, there was likewise no such sharp division between the clear day-consciousness and the unconsciousness of the night as appeared after the Atlantean period. During the night the astral body slipped out of the ether and physical bodies, but since the ether body still remained partly united with the astral body, there were always reflections of the spiritual world; the human being could always have a hazy clairvoyance, could live within the spiritual world and could behold about him spiritual beings and spiritual activities. The scholars who sit in their studies say that the common people have composed, for example, the Germanic myths and sagas out of their folk phantasy. Wotan and Thor and all the other gods were only personifications of nature forces. There are complete mythological theories which deal in this way with the folk creative phantasy. When one hears such a thing, it is easy to believe that such a learned individual is like the Homunculus in Goethe's Faust, born out of a retort, who had never seen a real human being. For anyone who has really observed the people, it is not possible to speak in this way of the creative folk imagination. The legends of the gods are nothing less than what remains of actual events which people of earlier ages really beheld clairvoyantly. This Wotan really existed. During the night human beings wandered about among the gods in the spiritual world and knew Wotan and Thor there as well as they knew people of flesh and blood like themselves here upon the earth. What primitive people of that age beheld, for a long time dimly and clairvoyantly, has now become the content of myth and saga, especially of those of the Germans.

People who at that time migrated from west to east into the regions later called Germany were those who had retained, more or less, some degree of clairvoyance and who were still able at a certain time to perceive in the spiritual world. And simultaneously with the migrations of that greatest of initiates and his followers into Tibet, whence he sent forth the first cultural colony into India, initiates who fostered the Spiritual Life in the Mysteries were left behind everywhere among the people of Europe. Mysteries existed among these people, the Druid Mysteries, for example, but men no longer have any knowledge of them—for what is recounted is merely fantastic rubbish. It is a significant fact that at that time when the higher worlds were mentioned among the Druids or among the peoples of the regions of western Russia and Scandinavia where the Mysteries of the Trotts existed, there was always a large number who knew of these spiritual worlds. When they spoke of Wotan or of the incidents that occurred between Baldur and Hodur, they were not talking of something wholly unknown to them. There were many who had themselves experienced such incidents in special states of consciousness, and those not having the experiences themselves heard it from their neighbour in whom they had confidence. Wherever you might have gone in Europe, you would still have found vivid memories of what existed on Atlantis. What did exist there? Something one might call a natural, living companionship with the beings of the spiritual world, with what is today called Heaven. The human being continually entered into the spiritual world and lived there. In other words he needed no special religion to point out to him the existence of a spirit-land. What is the meaning of "religion"? It signifies *union,* union of the physical world with the spiritual. At that time the human being needed no special means of union with the spiritual world, because for him it was a world of natural experience. Just as there is no need now for anyone to impart to you a belief in the flowers of the field or in the beasts of the forest, because you see them with your own eyes, so similarly the Atlanteans "believed" in the gods and spiritual beings, not through religion, but because they experienced them. As human evolution progressed, mankind acquired a clear day-consciousness. It was in the post-Atlantean age that people acquired this clear *waking* consciousness and they gained it by renouncing their ancient *clairvoyant* consciousness. It will be theirs again in the future in addition to the present clear day-consciousness. For our ancestors here in Europe, the sagas and myths often aroused memory-pictures of the distant past. One might ask, what was the nature of these most developed human beings? Strange as it may sound, these highly developed individuals whom the leader guided eastward into Tibet were for the most part advanced, because they had lost their ancient, dreamlike consciousness. What does it signify to progress from the fourth over into the fifth root-race? It means becoming day-conscious; it means losing the ancient clairvoyance. The great initiate and guide led away the members of his little group in order that they might not have to live among people who were still at the stage of the ancient Atlanteans. Among the first, only those could be guided into the higher worlds who had been trained artificially, who had gone artificially through an occult training. It may be asked, what did the people of the first post-Atlantean epoch have left of that ancient relationship with the spiritual, divine world? Only the longing for the spirit world, the door to which had been closed. They felt that there had been a time—for they heard it in their sagas—when their forefathers had gazed into the spirit world, had lived there among spirits and gods and had discovered themselves in the midst of deep spiritual realities. "Oh, could we but experience this too!" they said and out of this longing the ancient Indian way of initiation was created. This method of initiation arose out of the longing for what was past and caused the pupil to lose, for a time, the clear day-consciousness which he had acquired in order that he might force himself back in consciousness to his former state. "Yoga" is the method of the ancient Indian initiation which, through its technique and exercises, restored what had been lost in a quite natural way.

Imagine, for example, an ancient Atlantean whose ether head protruded far beyond his physical head. When the astral body withdrew, a large part of the ether head was still united with it, therefore what it experienced could be imprinted upon the ether body and thus he became conscious of his experiences. When, in the last part of the Atlantean period, the ether part of the head was drawn wholly into the physical head, the astral body left the ether body entirely each night. Thus in the ancient initiations, the teacher had to try to draw out the ether body of his pupil by artificial means; in other words, the pupil had to be brought into a sort of lethargic condition, into a kind of death-like sleep which lasted about three and a half days. During this time the ether body protruded from the physical body and was loosened from it. What the astral body then experienced was impressed upon the ether body. Then when the ether body was re-drawn into the physical body, the pupil knew what he had experienced in the spiritual world.

That was the ancient method of initiation, the Yoga initiation, by means of which the pupil was lifted out of the world wherein he found himself in order to be transported back again into the spiritual world. And the cultural mood which resulted from this kind of initiation found its echo in the later Indian culture. It was this mood that gave rise to the words: Truth, Reality, Being exist only in the spiritual world, in that world into which a person enters when he lifts himself out of the physical sense-world. Here he is in the midst of the physical world, surrounded by the mineral, plant and animal kingdoms. But what surrounds him is not reality, it is only an outer semblance; he lost the reality ages ago and now lives in a world of appearance, of illusion, of Maya!

The world of the physical, therefore, was the world of Maya for the ancient Indian civilization. We must comprehend this, not as a dull theory, but in accordance with the cultural mood itself—in accordance with the feelings of the people themselves of that time. When the ancient Indian wished to be especially holy, the world of illusion became worthless to him. This physical world became to him an illusion; the true world existed for him when he withdrew from the physical, when through Yoga he was permitted to live again in the world in which his forefathers still lived during the Atlantean period.

The significance of further evolution consists in the human being of this post-Atlantean period becoming gradually accustomed to value the physical world which is allotted to him, according to its worth and meaning. The second epoch, the next step after the ancient Indian period, is also a pre-historic cultural epoch which is named after the people who later lived in the region of Persia; we designate it the primitive Persian civilization. However, we have not the later Persian civilization in mind, but a pre-historic culture.

The second period differs very essentially in its mood, in its feeling-content from the primeval Indian period. It became more and more difficult to loosen the ether body during initiation, but it was still possible and in a certain way it was always done even up to the time of Christ-Jesus. But there was one thing these men of the primitive Persian civilization had attained; they began to appreciate Maya or illusion as something of value. The ancient Indian was happy when he could flee from illusion. For the Persian, it became a sphere of activity. It is true, illusion still continued to appear to him as something hostile, something which must be overcome. Later this gave rise to the myth of the battle between *Ormuzd* and *Ahriman* in which the human being allied himself with the good gods against the power of the gods of evil existing in matter. Out of this, the mood of that age was created. The Persian was still not fond of this physical "reality" (Maya), but he no longer fled from it like the ancient Indian; he worked upon it and considered it a stage upon which he could be active, a place where there was something that must be overcome. In this second cultural stage, a step in the conquest of the physical world had been made.

Then came the third cultural stage. We are now approaching closer and closer to historical times. This cultural period is designated in Occult Science the Chaldaic-Babylonian-Assyrian-Egyptian civilization. All these civilizations were founded by colonies sent out under the guidance of great leaders. The first colony founded the civilization of the ancient Indians, the second founded what we have just described as the ancient

Persian cultural centre and a third cultural stream travelled still further to the west and laid there the foundation of the Babylonian - Chaldaic - Assyrian - Egyptian civilization. Thus an important step was taken in the conquest of the physical world. To the Persian it still seemed like an intractable mass which he had to manipulate if he wished to work in it with those Beings whom he considered the good Spirits of the true Spiritual Reality. He had now become more familiar, more intimate with physical reality. Just consider the ancient Chaldean astronomy. It is one of the most extraordinary and tremendous creations of the human spirit of the post-Atlantean age. There you see how the course of the stars was explored, how the laws of the heavens were examined. The ancient Indian would have looked out at this heaven and said: The course of the stars with its laws is not worth the trouble to investigate! To the people of the third cultural epoch it was even then very important to penetrate into these laws. To those belonging to the Egyptian civilization, it was of special importance to examine the earthly relationships and to develop the science of geometry. Maya or illusion was explored and physical science came into being. Men studied the thoughts of the gods and felt that they must make a connection between their own individual activity and what they found inscribed in matter as the script of the gods. If you were to investigate spiritually the earlier conditions of Egyptian political life, you would gain a concept of a political organism very different from any that people of the present day can possibly imagine. The individualities who directed and guided those political states were wise men who knew the laws governing the course of the stars, of the movements of the cosmic bodies, and at the same time they knew that everything in the cosmos must mutually correspond. They had studied the course of the stars and knew that there must be a harmony between what was taking place in the heavens and what was happening upon the earth. According to the events in the heavens they decreed what, in the course of time, is to occur on earth. Even in the earliest part of the Roman period (the fourth cultural epoch) there still existed the consciousness that what transpires upon the earth must correspond to what is happening in the heavens. For long periods in the ancient Mysteries it was known at the beginning of a new epoch what events would transpire in the following period. It was known through the Mystery-wisdom, for example, at the beginning of Roman history that a period would follow in which the most varied historical events would be enacted and that they would take place in the region of Alba Longa. For anyone who can read it, it is clear that a deeply symbolical expression is suggested here and that it was, so to say, priestly wisdom that laid out or planned the civilization of ancient Rome. "Alba Longa" was the long priestly garment. In these ancient regions the future historical events were in this way laid out—if we may be allowed to use a technical expression. They knew that seven epochs must follow one after another in succession. The future was divided according to the number seven and an outline of the future history was foretold. I could easily show you how prophetic historical plans were concealed in the story of the seven Kings of Rome which had already been inscribed in the *Sibylline Books* even as early as the beginning of the Roman epoch. In those days people knew that they had to live through what was written there and on important occasions they consulted the Holy Books. This then accounts for the holy and mysterious character of the *Sibylline Books*.

Thus humanity of the third cultural epoch worked Spirit into Matter, permeated the outer world with Spirit. There are countless historical evidences of this concealed in the development of the epochs of this third cultural stream—this Assyrian - Babylonian - Chaldean - Egyptian civilization. Our own age can be understood only when we know the important relationships which exist between that age and our own. I should like now to call attention to one of the relationships between these two epochs, in order that you may see how wonderfully things are connected for anyone who can penetrate more deeply into them and who knows that what is called egotism and utilitarianism has now reached its culmination. Never before was a cultural epoch as purely egotistic and unidealistic as our own and it will become even more so in the near future. For, at the present time, spirit has descended completely into a materialistic civilization. Tremendous spiritual forces have had to be employed by men in the great discoveries and inventions of the new age, that is, of the nineteenth century. Just think, for instance, how much spiritual force exists in the telephone, in the telegraph, in the railroads, etc.! How much spiritual force has been materialized, crystallized in the commercial relationships of the earth! How much spiritual energy it requires to cause a sum of money to be paid, let us say in Tokyo, by means of a piece of paper, a cheque written here in this place! Thus one may ask: Does the use of this spiritual force mean spiritual progress? Whoever faces the fact must acknowledge the following: You build railroads indeed, but they carry, practically, only what you need for your stomachs; and when you yourself travel, you do so only because of something that has to do with your physical needs. Does it make any difference from the standpoint of Spiritual Science whether we grind our own corn with a few stones or obtain it from a distance by means of the telegraph, ships, etc.? A tremendous spiritual force is employed, but it is used in an entirely personal sense. What then will be the meaning of what men thus negotiate? Apparently not Anthroposophy, in other words, not spiritual realities. When the telegraph and steamships are used, it is in the first place a question of how much cotton will be ordered to be sent from America to Europe, etc.; in other words it is a question of something that has to do with personal needs. Mankind has descended to the profoundest depths of personal necessity, of physical personality. But just such an egotistic, utilitarian principle had to come sometime, because through it, the ascending course of all human evolution will be facilitated. What has happened to cause the human being to attach so much importance to his own personality, thus causing him to feel himself so much a separate individual? And, moreover, what was it that prepared him for this strong feeling of self in his life between birth and death?

In the third period of civilization a most important preparation was made for this, in the desire to retain the form of the physical body beyond death in the "mummy," in the wish to prevent the dissipation of the form of the body by embalming it. Thus, this holding fast to the separate individuality became imprinted upon the soul in such a way that now it appears again in another incarnation as the feeling of personality. That this feeling of personality is so strong today is the result of the embalming of the body in the Egyptian period. So we see that in human evolution everything is correlated. The Egyptians mummified the bodies of the dead in order that people of the fifth epoch might have the greatest possible consciousness of their own personality. Certainly, profound mysteries exist within human evolution.

Thus you see how the human being has gradually descended deeper and deeper into Maya and has permeated matter with what he is able to achieve. In the fourth cultural period, the Greco-Latin age, he placed his inner being out in the external world. Thus you see in Greece how he objectified himself in matter and form. He concealed his own form in the figures of the Grecian gods. In Aeschylos there still resounds, in dramatic form, men's desire to convert their own individuality into artistic form. They step out upon the physical plane and create a copy of themselves. In the Roman period men created an image of themselves in the institutions of the State. It is a sign of the greatest dilletantism when one traces what is now called Jurisprudence back beyond the Roman period. What existed previously is, in concept, something quite different from *Jus* or "Justice," "Right" (*Recht*), for the concept of the human being as an outer personality, the concept of human rights did not exist prior to that time. In ancient Greece there was the *Polis*, the little municipal state, and men felt themselves as members of it. It is difficult for people to enter into the consciousness of the Greek epoch. In the Roman epoch, the path into the physical world had been trod so far that the individual human personality—as a Roman citizen—appears also as possessing rights. Everything progresses by stages and we shall trace in detail how the personality emerges by degrees and how at the same time the physical world is being conquered more and more in the progress of history, and how the human being is plunging deeper and deeper into matter.

Our own epoch is the first after the Greco-Latin; in other words, it is the fifth epoch of the post-Atlantean age. There will follow after it a sixth and a seventh epoch. The fourth, the Greco-Latin, is the middle period, and during this *middle* period, *Christ-Jesus* came upon the earth. This event was prepared for within the third post-Atlantean epoch, because everything in the world has to be prepared beforehand. The third epoch made ready for that greatest of all events which was to be enacted upon the earth during the fourth post-Atlantean epoch at a time when men had progressed far enough in their feeling of personality to step outside themselves and create their gods in their own image. In the art of the Grecian period, men created a world of gods after their own image. They repeated this in the form of the State. An understanding of physical matter was reached even to the degree of the union of Maya (the world of illusion, matter) and Spirit. This is the moment when men also attained an understanding of personality. You will comprehend that this was also the time when they were able to understand God as a personal manifestation, the time when the spirit belonging to the earth also progressed to the point of becoming a personality. Thus we see how in the middle of the post-Atlantean civilization God Himself appeared as a man, as a separate personality. When we see how in Greek art the human being fashioned an image of himself, we may say: What happened in the middle of the post-Atlantean civilization appears to us as an image. When we pass from the Greek to the Roman period and observe the types of human beings of the great Roman Empire, does it not actually seem as though the Greek images of the gods had descended from their pedestals and were walking about in their togas? One can fairly see them!

Thus the human creature had progressed from the time when he felt himself as a member of the Godhead to a feeling of himself as a personality. He could comprehend as a personality even the Godhead Itself which, embodied in the flesh, had descended and dwelt among men.

It has been our desire here to picture to our souls the reason for the appearance of Christ-Jesus just at this period of human evolution. How this mystery developed further, how in the earlier evolutionary periods it shone forth prophetically, and how it works prophetically into the distant future, we shall consider next time.

IX

THE PROPHETICAL DOCUMENTS
and
THE ORIGIN OF CHRISTIANITY

During the whole course of our lectures, you have seen what our position is in relation to the document called the Gospel of St. John, standing as we do upon the foundation of Spiritual Science. You have seen that it is not a question of gaining out of this document some particular truths about the spiritual world, but of showing that, independent of all human and other documents, it is possible to penetrate into that world, just as anyone wishing to learn mathematics at present does so independent of every original document by means of which, in the course of human evolution, different branches of mathematics have first been communicated. What, for example, do those students know who begin to study elementary geometry, acquiring it by means of their own faculties from geometry itself, what do they know of the geometry of Euclid, of the original document in which this elementary geometry was presented to the world for the first time? If the student has first learned geometry by means of his own faculties, he can judge and appreciate better the nature and meaning of the original documents. This should show us more and more that those truths which deal with this spiritual life can be gained out of the life of the spirit itself. If a person has found these truths for himself and then is directed to the historical documents, he finds in them again what he already knows. In this way he acquires a right and true human valuation of them. We have seen in the course of these lectures, that the Gospel of St. John really loses nothing in value by this method; we have seen that the respect for and appreciation of documents do not become less for anyone standing upon the foundation of Spiritual Science than for those who have stood entirely upon the foundation of such documents. Indeed, we have seen that we find again in the Gospel of St. John the most profound teaching concerning Christianity, a teaching which we can also call the teaching of Universal Wisdom. We have also seen that only when we have grasped this profound meaning of the Christian teaching, can we understand why the Christ had to enter into human evolution just at a definite time at the beginning of our era.

We have seen how humanity developed in the post-Atlantean age. It has been pointed out that the original Indian civilization was the first great post-Atlantean cultural epoch after the Atlantean Flood; that the characteristic of this original Indian civilization was that the souls of men were filled with longing and memory. We have characterized memory and longing by saying that they consisted in the preservation of living traditions from an epoch of human evolution ante-dating the Atlantean Flood. At that time, quite in conformity with their nature and inner being, men existed in a kind of nebulous, clairvoyant state in which they could gaze into the spiritual world, thus becoming acquainted with it through personal experience and knowledge, just as men of the present time are acquainted with the four kingdoms of nature, the mineral, plant, animal and human kingdoms. We have seen that prior to the Atlantean Flood, there existed as yet no such sharp distinction as we have today between the states of consciousness during the day and the night. At that time, when the human being sank into sleep at night, his inner experiences were not so unconscious and dark as they are now, for when the images of day life submerged, those of the spiritual life emerged, and he was then in the midst of the things of the spirit world. In the morning, when he again dipped down into his physical body, the experiences and realities of the divine-spiritual world sank into darkness, and around him arose the images of present reality, images of the present mineral, plant and animal kingdoms. The sharp distinction between the unconsciousness of the night and day waking-consciousness appeared only after the Atlantean Flood, that is to say, in our post-Atlantean age. Then, in a certain sense, as far as direct perception is concerned, men were cut off from spiritual reality and were more and more placed outside in purely physical reality. All that remained was the memory of the existence of another kingdom, a kingdom of spiritual beings, and united with this memory was the soul's longing to rise again by means of some exceptional condition into the regions out of which it had descended. Those exceptional conditions were only granted to a few chosen people—the initiates —whose inner faculties had been awakened in the Mystery Places enabling them to gaze into the spiritual world; to those others who were not able

to do this, these initiates were able to give information about that world
and testify to its reality. In the original Indian cultural period, Yoga was
the process by which men were able to revert to the ancient nebulous,
clairvoyant state of consciousness. When certain exceptional natures were
initiated, they became, as a result, the leaders of mankind, witnesses of
the spiritual world.

Under the effect of this longing and memory within this original
Indian, pre-Vedic civilization, that soul-mood was particularly developed
which regarded physical reality as Maya or illusion. These primitive
Indian people said that actual reality exists alone in the spiritual world
into which we can be reinstated only by means of an exceptional condition, through Yoga. This world of spiritual beings and processes is the
true one. What is seen with the eyes, is unreal, is illusion, Maya. That
was the first religious fundamental experience of the post-Atlantean age,
and Yoga was the first form of initiation of this period. In fact there was
yet no comprehension of the true mission of the post-Atlantean age. For
it was not the mission of humanity to consider the reality, which we call
physical existence, as Maya or illusion and then to flee from it and become
foreign to it. Post-Atlantean humanity had another mission, that of conquering more and more the physical reality, of becoming master of the
world of physical phenomena. But it is also quite comprehensible that
men, now for the first time transferred to this physical plane, should in
the beginning consider as Maya or illusion what previously had hardly
emerged within the spiritual reality, but what was now all that they were
able to perceive. This attitude toward reality could never have continued.
This understanding of the physical reality as an illusion could not remain
the vital nerve of the post-Atlantean period. And we have seen that post-
Atlantean humanity, in the different cultural epochs, conquered bit by bit
the connection with the physical reality.

In that period of civilization which we designate the ancient Persian
—the periods which history knows as the Persian and Zarathustrian
periods are the last echoes of what is meant here—in that second period,
we saw mankind taking the first step toward growing out of the ancient
Indian principle and conquering physical reality. Still nowhere was
there a fondness for sinking into the physical reality, also there existed
nowhere anything like a study of the physical world. There was, how-

ever, more of this in the Persian period than in the ancient Indian period. We get a reverberation of the mood that looks upon physical reality as illusion in what has survived in later epochs of ancient Indian civilization. Yet our present civilization could never have arisen out of that Indian culture. All the wisdom of that period turned its gaze away from the physical world and directed it upward toward spiritual worlds which existed as a memory. The study of physical reality and its elaboration seemed to them futile, therefore the actual Indian principle could never have brought forth a science serviceable to our earthly world; it could never have produced that mastery of the laws of nature which forms the foundation of our present civilization. This could never have sprung from ancient India, for why should one seek to learn to know the forces of a world resting only upon illusion! If this was changed in the Indian cultural period also, it was not because of something flowing out of itself, but was due to subsequent foreign influences.

For the ancient Persian civilization, the external, physical reality exists as a sphere of activity. It was looked upon as the expression of a hostile Deity, but the hope arose that with the aid of the God of Light this substantial field of reality might be penetrated, that it might be changed into something permeated by spiritual powers and good divinities. Thus the adherents of the Persian civilization already sensed somewhat the reality of the physical world. It is true they still considered it the realm of the God of Darkness, but for all that, they always hoped that they might be able to incorporate within it the forces of the good gods.

Humanity then passed over into that period of civilization which found its historical expression in the Babylonian-Assyrian-Chaldaic-Egyptian culture and we have seen how it happened that the starry heavens were no longer Maya to these people of the third epoch, but something whose written characters could be read. In all that still seemed a Maya to the Indians in the course and splendour of the stars, the Persian saw an expression of the resolutions and purposes of divine-spiritual beings. They gradually accustomed themselves to the idea that outer reality is not illusion but a revelation, a manifestation of divine-spiritual beings. Then in the Egyptian civilization, men began to apply what they read in the stars to the divisions of the earth. Why was it the Egyptians became the masters of Geometry? It was because they believed that through thought, which subdivides the earth, matter can also be controlled, and that matter, which can be grasped by the human spirit, is easily transformed. Thus gradually a later humanity permeated this material world—looked upon at first as only Maya—with the spirit, and this spirit also gradually emerged within the inner soul life of the human being.

We have seen, in fact, that only in the later Atlantean age, humanity had reached the point where it could experience the ego or the "I AM." For as long as men beheld spiritual images, they knew that they themselves belonged to the spiritual world, that they were themselves images among other images. Then came a comprehension of the spirit within the depths of the human being. Let us now consider, in connection with what we have partially reviewed today, the evolution of the inner nature of men.

As long as the human being of the Atlantean period looked outward with a kind of dream-like, clairvoyant consciousness he did not really give much attention to his own inner nature. The inner world, which is encompassed by the ego or the "I AM," was not yet delineated in sharp contours. In proportion as the outer spiritual world disappeared, men became conscious of their own inner world of the spirit. In the ancient Indian civilization there still existed in the individual an extraordinary attitude of soul toward his own spiritual life. People said: If we wish to penetrate into the spiritual world, to raise ourselves above illusion, we must lose ourselves in the spiritual world, we must obliterate as much as possible the "I AM" and become absorbed into the All-Spirit, into Brahman. Thus especially in ancient initiation, it was a matter of a loss of personality. An impersonal absorption into the spiritual world is what distinguished the most ancient form of initiation. This was no longer so, for example, in the third epoch of civilization, for right up to that time the human *self-consciousness* had by degrees been developing stronger and stronger. The human being became continually more and more conscious within the inner part of his ego being. By developing a fondness for the physical matter about him, by deepening his knowledge of it by means of the laws which the human spirit had thought out, but which had not been acquired in any sort of shadowy dream-state, he became gradually more aware of his ego, until this consciousness of personality reached a certain high point in the ancient Egyptian civilization. In this awareness of the personality, there was present something else that appeared at the same time inferior and as though now bound to the physical world and absorbed into it, something that had no possibility of acquiring a connection with that from which the human being had been born.

If we wish to grasp the whole course of events, we must picture to our souls two fundamental soul-moods in human evolution. We must remember how humanity of the Atlantean and ancient Indian periods longed to strip off personality. The Atlanteans were able to accomplish this, and they took it for granted that they would each night strip off their personality and live in the land of the spirit. The Indians could do this, because their principle of initiation led them, by means of their Yoga, into what was impersonal. To repose in the universal divine substance was their desire. In a later branch of the human family, this reposing within the universal was preserved in the consciousness of being united with preceding generations. It remained in the consciousness of the people that they had been born out of a line of ancestry, and an individual human being felt himself united through the blood with generations as far back as his earliest ancestor. This was the mood which grew out of that ancient soul-mood of feeling oneself spiritually sheltered within the divine-spiritual substance. Thus it happened that those human beings who had passed through a normal evolution began in the third cultural epoch to feel themselves as individuals, yet, at the same time, knowing that they were sheltered within the whole, within the divine-spiritual, that they belonged through the blood relationship to the entire line of forefathers, and that God lived for them in the blood flowing down to them through the generations. We have seen how a certain degree of perfection of this mood had been developed within those people who composed the followers of the Old Testament. "I and Father Abraham are one," means that the individual felt himself preserved within the whole line of descent back to Abraham. That was, in general, what constituted the fundamental mood of all normally developed races of the third cultural period. However, only to the followers of the Old Testament was it predicted that there existed something spiritually more profound than the Divine Fatherhood that ran through the blood of successive generations. We have already called attention to that great moment in human evolution when this was prophesied. When Moses heard the voice calling unto him saying: "When thou wouldst proclaim My Name, say that 'I AM' hath said it unto thee!", then here for the first time sounds forth the knowledge and manifestation of the Logos, of the Christ. Here for the first time, for those who could comprehend, was prophetically proclaimed that in God there existed something that not only had to do with the blood relationship, but that in Him there existed something purely spiritual. What ran through the Old Testament was like a prophecy. Who was it, in fact, who at that time in a prophecy revealed His name to Moses? We must now dwell a little on this question. Here again we have a passage which the commentators of the Gospel consider very superficially, not recognizing the fact that one must examine these records as thoroughly as possible.

Who was it who announced His name prophetically, to Whom the name "I AM" must be given? Who was it? We find the answer, if with earnestness and dignity we properly grasp a certain passage of the Gospel. It is the passage which we find in the 12th Chapter, beginning with the 37th verse. Here Christ-Jesus points to the fulfilment of the words of the Prophet Isaiah, to the prophecy with its reference to the fact that the Jews would not believe in Christ-Jesus. Jesus Himself refers to Isaiah:

He hath blinded their eyes and hardened their hearts, that they should not see with their eyes nor understand with their hearts and be converted and I should heal them.

These things said Isaiah when he saw His glory and spake with Him.

Isaiah *spake with Him!* With *Whom* did Isaiah speak? Reference is made here to the passage in Isaiah 6, 1 which reads:

In the year that the King of Uzziah died, I saw also the Lord sitting upon a throne high and lifted up and His train filled the Temple.

Whom did Isaiah see? This is clearly told here in the Gospel of St. John. He saw the Christ! He was always to be seen in the spirit and now you will no longer find it incomprehensible when Spiritual Science points out that He whom Moses saw, who proclaimed the words "I AM" as His name, was the same Being who then appeared upon the earth as the Christ. The actual Spirit of God of antiquity is none other than the Christ. We are now at a point in this religious record which is very difficult to understand, especially for those who do not go at it properly. This passage must be clearly understood, particularly because with the words Father, Son, and Holy Spirit, the most extraordinary confusion has arisen. It is a fact that exoterically these words have always been used in the most manifold ways in order that the real esoteric meaning might not be directly evident. When, according to ancient Judaism, the "father" was mentioned, the physical father whose blood flowed down through the generations was meant. When they spoke of Him who revealed Himself spiritually, as Isaiah spoke of the "Lord," they were referring to the Logos of which the Gospel of St. John speaks. The writer of this Gospel means nothing more nor less than that the One who could always be perceived in the spirit became flesh and dwelt among us!

When it has become clear to us that in a certain sense the Christ was also spoken of in the Old Testament, we shall understand what place the ancient Hebrew peoples have held in our evolution. The ancient Hebrew-principle grew out of the Egyptian civilization. It stands out in bold relief against the background of the Egyptian principle.

Thus we see how the normal course of human evolution progressed as it was described yesterday. The first cultural period of the post-Atlantean age is the ancient Indian, the second the ancient Persian, the third the Babylonian-Assyrian-Chaldaic-Egyptian civilization; then follows the fourth, the Greco-Latin and the fifth which is our own present cultural epoch. Before the fourth epoch began, that people which with its traditions provided the soil for Christianity emerged out of the third epoch like a mysterious branch. When we summarize all that we have been hearing in these lectures, we shall find it much more comprehensible that the appearance of the Christ had to take place in the fourth era.

We have already emphasized the fact that in the fourth epoch the human being had reached the point where he objectified his own spirituality, his own ego and had placed it out in the world. We perceive how gradually he permeated matter with his own spirit, with his ego-spirit. We behold the works of the Greek sculptors, and dramatists and see how they have presented, embodied before the soul, what they call their own soul qualities. Later, in the Roman period, we see how the human being also becomes conscious of what he is, and we see how he established this in the outer world as "Justice" (*Jus*), although a distorted Jurisprudence disguised it. For the deeper students of Jurisprudence, it is clear that real justice, which considers the human being its subject, first arose in this fourth cultural epoch. At that time the people had become conscious enough of their own personality to feel themselves for the first time as real citizens of the State. Even in the Greek period, the individual felt himself as a member of the whole municipal State. This was more important to an Athenian than to be an individual man. But to say "I am a Roman" or "I am an Athenian" meant two very different things. For to say, "I am a Roman" meant that, as an individual human being, as a citizen of the State, he had an importance, he had a will. Thus it could also be proven that the origin of the concept of a "testament" first became possible in this epoch, for this is a Roman concept. Only at that time did the human being make his will so personal, so individualized, that he wished to be active in it even beyond death. The things which Spiritual Science has to say harmonize even in the details with the actual facts.

The human being gradually reached the point of permeating matter with his spirit and this increased as time went on. The fourth epoch was that in which he thoroughly incorporated into matter what he comprehended with his spirit. In the Egyptian Pyramids you can see how spirit and matter are still wrestling with one another, how what had been grasped by the spirit had not yet fully expressed itself in matter. In the Greek Temple is expressed the complete turning point of the post-Atlantean age. For one who understands a little of this, there is no more significant, no more perfect architecture than the Greek which is the purest expression of the inner characteristic of *space*. The pillars are considered wholly as supports, and what rests upon them is felt as something that must be supported, something that presses down. The supreme, emancipated concept of space is here in the Greek Temple carried to its ultimate conclusions. Few people have subsequently felt the concept of space in this way, yet there have been those who could have felt it, but they felt it *pictorially*. Let anyone test the space in the Sistine Chapel. Stand at the rear wall which bears the great picture of the Last Judgment, and look up. You will see that the rear wall rises obliquely upward. It inclines thus because the architect *felt* the concept of space, but did not *think* it so abstractly as others. Therefore this wall stands there so marvellously at an angle. This means that he no longer experienced the concept of space as did the Greeks. There is an artistic sense which feels the mysterious measure concealed in space. To sense it architecturally does not mean to sense it by means of the eyes, but by means of something else. People easily believe today that right is the same as left, above the same as below, forward the same as backward. If one would only consider the following: There are pictures in which three, four or five angels can be seen floating about. They can be painted in such a way that one would be right in thinking that they are in danger of falling at any moment. They can likewise be painted by someone who has developed the right sense for space, in such a manner that there is no possibility of such a thought arising; they could not fall because they mutually support each other. We then have the dynamic relationships in space pictorially represented before us. The Greeks had it *architecturally* before them. They experienced the horizontal not alone as line, but as the force of pressure and they experienced the pillar not only as a block of something, but as supporting power. This *feeling-with-the-lines-of-space* means, "feeling the living Spirit in the act of geometrizing." That is what Plato meant when he used the tremendous expression, "God geometrizes continually."

These lines really exist in space and the Greeks built their Temples in accordance with them. What was in reality a Greek Temple? From necessity it was the dwelling-house of their God. It was something quite different from the Church of the present day. The present Church is a place for preaching. The God Himself dwelt within the Greek Temple. The people were only present incidentally when they wished to be with their God. One who understands the forms of the Greek Temple, experiences a mysterious connection with the God dwelling within it. There, in the columns, and in what rests upon them, is to be seen not only what the human being has fashioned in imagination, but something that his God would have thus made, had He wished to create a dwelling place for Himself. This was the climax of the permeation of Matter with Spirit.

Let us now compare a Greek Temple with a Gothic Church. Nothing derogatory of the Gothic is intended, for from another point of view the

Gothic Church stands upon a still higher level than the Greek Temple. In a Gothic Church you can see that what is expressed in its form cannot possibly be thought of or felt without the presence of the devotional congregation. In the arched forms of the Gothic there exists something (for one who can experience it) which can only be expressed in the following words: If the devotional congregation were not within, and the hands were not placed together in the form of an arch, the whole would be incomplete. The Gothic Church is not only the dwelling-house of God, but it is at the same time the meeting place for people who are praying to God. Thus, in a certain sense, mankind again over-stepped the zenith of its own evolution. We see how all that degenerated which the Greeks felt in line, column and beam in such a remarkable manner through their sense of space. A column which does not support, but which is there only as a decorative motif, was for the Greek feeling no column at all. Everything in human evolution is in perfect accord. The Greek cultural period was the most beautiful expression of the interpenetration of humanity's consciousness discovered within itself, and of what was felt as the Divine in outer space. The human being had wholly coalesced with the physical sense-world in this epoch.

It is nonsense when modern scholars wish to obscure what was felt in earlier ages. From the Spiritual-Scientific point of view, we look upon the fourth epoch of the post-Atlantean age as an epoch in which the human being harmonized perfectly with his environment. That age—in which he seemed to coalesce with the outer reality—was alone qualified to understand that the Divine is able to appear in an individual man. All earlier epochs would have understood almost anything more easily than this. They would have felt that the Divine was much too exalted and sublime to appear in a physical human form. It was just this physical form against which they desired to guard the Divine. Therefore, "Thou shalt make no image" had to be announced to just that people whose mission it was to grasp the idea of God in His spiritual form. Out of concepts such as these, this people evolved and out .of its womb was begotten the idea of the Christ, the idea that spirit was to appear in the flesh. For this mission was the Jewish people chosen and within it, in the fourth post-Atlantean epoch, the Christ Event had to occur.

Thus for the Christian consciousness, the whole of human existenc(

falls into a pre-Christian and a post-Christian period. The God-Man could only be comprehended by the human being at a certain time. Thus we see how the Gospel of St. John connects in full consciousness and in its ideas, with what was—to use a trivial expression—precisely in conformity with the times, with what had its origin directly in the consciousness of the age. Consequently it happened wholly of itself, that the thought imagery, through which the writer of the Gospel tried to grasp the greatest event in cosmic history, seemed to him best expressed in the forms of Greek thought, as it were, like something inwardly related. And gradually the whole Christian feeling grew into these thought forms. We shall see how something like the Gothic had to appear during the progress of evolution, because Christianity was, as it were, called upon to lead evolution again beyond the material. Christianity could arise only at a time when men were not yet so deeply immersed in matter that they were likely to overestimate its worth; when they were not yet plunged so deeply into matter as is the case in our age, but were still able to spiritualize it and to penetrate it.

Thus the birth of Christianity appears as something positively necessary in the whole spiritual course of human events. If we desire to understand what form Christianity should gradually assume, understand what form was prophesied for it by such an individuality as the writer of this Gospel, we must take under consideration, in the next lecture, certain essential and important concepts.

It has been shown that everything must be taken literally, but that first the alphabet must be really understood. It is not without significance that the name of John appears nowhere in the Gospel and that John is always spoken of as the "Disciple whom the Lord loved." We have seen what mystery lies hidden behind this fact, a mystery of profound significance.

Now we shall consider another expression, one that makes it directly possible for us to make a connection with the subsequent evolutionary periods of Christianity. The manner of speaking of the "Mother of Jesus" in the Gospel, is usually overlooked. If the ordinary, average Christian were asked: who was the Mother of Jesus? he would reply: "The Mother of Jesus was Mary!" And many indeed will believe that there is something in the Gospel of St. John to the effect that the Mother of Jesus was called Mary. But nowhere in this Gospel is there anything to indicate that the Mother of Jesus was called Mary. Wherever reference is made to her, she is quite intentionally called just the Mother of Jesus. The meaning of this we shall learn later. In the chapter on the Marriage in Cana, we read: "and the Mother of Jesus was there;" and further on, it says: "His Mother saith unto the servants." Nowhere do we find the name "Mary." And when we meet her again in the Gospel of St. John, when we see the Saviour upon the Cross, we read:

"There stood by the Cross of Jesus, His Mother, and His Mother's sister Mary, the wife of Cleophas, and Mary Magdalene."

It is clearly and definitely stated who stood by the Cross. The Mother was there, then her sister who was the wife of Cleophas and who was called Mary, and Mary Magdalene. Whoever thinks about it at all, must say to himself: It is extraordinary that the two sisters are both called Mary! That is not customary in our day. It was also not customary at that time. And since the writer of the Gospel calls the sister, Mary, it is clear that the Mother of Jesus was not called Mary. In the Greek text, it says clearly and distinctly: "Below stood the Mother of Jesus, and His Mother's sister Mary who was the wife of Cleophas, and Mary Magdalene." For a proper understanding the question arises: "Who was the Mother of Jesus?" Here we touch upon one of the most important questions in the Gospel of St. John: "Who was the real father of Jesus, and who was His mother?"

Who was the father? Can this question be asked at all? Not only can it be asked according to the Gospel of St. John, but also according to St. Luke. For it would show an extraordinary absence of thought not to see that at the Annunciation it was proclaimed:

The Holy Ghost shall come upon thee, and the power of the Highest shall overshadow thee; therefore also, that holy thing which shall be born of thee shall be called the Son of God.

Even in the Gospel of St. Luke it is pointed out that the father of Jesus is the Holy Spirit. This must be taken literally and those theologians who do not recognize it cannot really read the Gospel. Thus we must ask the great question:—How does all this harmonize with what we have heard in the words, "I and the Father are one," "I and Father Abraham are one," "Before Abraham was, was the I AM"? How can we bring into harmony with all this, the undeniable fact that the Evangelist sees the Father-Principle in the Holy Spirit? And what must we think about the Mother-Principle, according to the Gospel of St. John?

In order that you may come tomorrow properly prepared in spirit to formulate these questions, your attention should also be called to the fact that a sort of series of generations is presented in the Gospel of St. Luke; that we are told that Jesus was baptized by John the Baptist; that He began to teach in His thirtieth year and that He was the son of "Mary and Joseph, who was the son of Eli," etc., and there follows the whole line of generations. If we trace this succession, we see that it goes back to Adam. Then follows something extraordinary; here we find the words: "who was the son of God." Just as the generations are traced back from son to father in the Gospel of St. Luke, so is the succession traced back from Adam to God. Such a passage must be taken very seriously! Now we have gathered together the questions which should lead us tomorrow directly into the very center of the Gospel of St. John.

X

THE EFFECT OF THE
CHRIST IMPULSE WITHIN MANKIND

We have been considering the whole law of evolution of the post-Atlantean humanity, and we have tried to understand why the founding of Christianity should have taken place just at a particular moment in this period of evolution. Yesterday at the close of our lecture, we observed that an understanding of important questions in the Gospel of St. John and in the whole of Christianity depends upon our keeping well in mind this evolutionary law in its esoteric, Christian sense. Only in this way shall we be able to gain a complete understanding of the meaning of the words "Holy Spirit," "Father and Mother of Jesus." Above all we must remember that in the course of the last lectures, it was made clear that the post-Atlantean humanity falls into seven sub-divisions. It is, in fact, that humanity to which, strictly speaking, we, ourselves belong and which developed after the Atlantean Flood. I intentionally avoided the idea of "sub-races," because the concept "race" does not fully coincide with the idea we are considering. What we are considering are cultural periods of development and what we still experience as racial laws in our present humanity is, in fact, an echo of the Atlantean evolution. The human evolution which preceded the Atlantean Flood, which took place for the most part upon a continent lying between present Europe and America, upon ancient Atlantis, can also be divided into seven successive groups. To these seven groups the expression "racial evolution" is applicable, for these seven successive stages of humanity upon ancient Atlantis differed widely from each other bodily, both internally and externally. We include in the external body also the inner configurations of brain, blood and other fluids. But it cannot be said that the earliest humanity of the post-Atlantean age, the Indian, differed sufficiently from ourselves for us to be able to employ the expression "race" for it. We must always hold fast to the continuity of Divine Wisdom, therefore it is often necessary to form a connection with this ancient concept of the race. Yet false ideas can very easily be created by this word "race" through our failing to see that the reason for the division of humanity of the present is something of a much more inner character than the idea usually attached to the word race. Race can no longer be used for the culture that will replace our own after the seventh subdivision, because then humanity will be divided according to quite different fundamental laws.

From this point of view we must consider the division of the post-Atlantean period into the following epochs: 1st the ancient Indian epoch; 2nd the ancient Persian; 3rd the Babylonian-Assyrian-Chaldean-Egyptian; 4th the Greco-Latin; and 5th, the epoch in which we now live. Our epoch will be replaced by a 6th and that by a 7th evolutionary epoch. We are now in the 5th post-Atlantean cultural epoch and say to ourselves:— Christianity entered into human evolution in its full profundity and significance in the 4th epoch. It has had its influence on the humanity of the 5th epoch to a marked degree and we shall now forecast prophetically what its further effect will be, as far as this is possible out of Spiritual Wisdom. We indicated yesterday that the mission of Christianity was prepared in the 3rd epoch. The Egyptian civilization belongs to the 3rd epoch, and out of its womb the adherents of the Old Testament directed the development of Hebrew culture in such a way that Christianity was born, as it were, coming fully into the world in the 4th epoch, in the person of Christ Jesus. We may say that humanity experienced a certain spiritual influence in the 3rd epoch of the post-Atlantean age. This worked on into the 4th Epoch, concentrating in the person of Christ Jesus, then continued on into the 5th, our own, and from thence it will work on over into the 6th epoch which will follow ours. Now we must clearly understand how all this has occurred.

Let us call to mind that in the course of human evolution, the various constituent parts of the human being have experienced their own evolution. Let us recall how it was in the later Atlantean period. We have described how the ether head sank into the physical body and how at that time people developed the rudimentary capacity for saying "I AM" to themselves. When the Atlantean Flood occurred, the human physical body was permeated by the power of the "I AM;" this means that human progress had advanced far enough to have prepared the physical instrument for the ego or for self-consciousness. By this we understand quite clearly that if we were to go back into the middle of the Atlantean period, we should find no human being in the position to develop a self-conscious-ness in which it was possible for him to speak the words, "I am an I" or "I AM," out of himself. That could only occur after that part of the ether head, of which we have spoken, has united with the physical part of the head. Up to the time of the submersion of Atlantis by the Flood, the human being had developed the rudiments of the physical brain, which was to become the bearer of this self-consciousness, and the germs of the other configurations of his physical body. Up to the time of the Atlantean Flood, the physical body was being made ready to be the bearer of the ego. We may ask: What was the mission of Atlantis? It was to implant the ego in the human being, to imprint it upon him, and this mission then reached out beyond the Flood—described as the Deluge—over into our age. In our post-Atlantean epoch, however, something else had to enter; gradually and by degrees, Manas or Spirit-Self had to enter into the human being. The influence of Manas or Spirit-Self begins with our post-Atlan-tean age. We know that after we have passed through various embodi-ments in our sixth or seventh epochs, Manas or Spirit-Self will have overshadowed us to a certain degree. But a longer preparation is needed for the human being to become a fit instrument for this Manas or Spirit-Self. Before that, he will first have to become a true bearer of the "I" or ego, even though it take thousands of years. He will not only have to make his physical body an instrument for the ego, but the other members of his being as well.

In the first cultural epoch of the post-Atlantean period, the human being for the first time made his ether body into a bearer of the ego, just as he had previously done with his physical body. This was the ancient Indian civilization. In this epoch, the human being acquired the ability to develop not only a physical instrument for the ego, but also a fitting ether body. Therefore in the following table, the first epoch, the ancient Indian civilization is indicated as having an ether body.

If we now wish to consider the further evolution of these cultural epochs in relation to the human being, we must not, merely superficially, consider the soul as the astral body, but we must proceed more accurately and take as a basis the membering of the human being which you will find in my book "Theosophy". You know that there we distinguish, in general,

(See diagram on following page)

PHYSICAL BODY	ATLANTIS	
ETHER BODY	1	POST-ATLANTEAN CULTURE EPOCH
SOUL BODY	2	CULTURE EPOCH
SENTIENT SOUL	3	CULTURE EPOCH
INTELLECTUAL SOUL	4	CULTURE EPOCH
CONSCIOUSNESS SOUL	5	CULTURE EPOCH
SPIRIT SELF	6	CULTURE EPOCH
LIFE SPIRIT	7	CULTURE EPOCH

SPIRIT SELF

) 1 DAY
) 2 DAY
) 3 DAY

LIFE SPIRIT

not only the seven human members, but the middle part we again divide into Soul Body, Sentient Soul, Intellectual Soul and Consciousness Soul—and then we have the higher members, Spirit-Self, Life-Spirit and Spirit-Man. Usually only seven members are to be distinguished. The fourth member which we summarize under the name "Ego," we must again divide, because in human evolution it is thus divided. What was evolved during the ancient Persian period is the actual Astral or Soul Body. It is the bearer of the actual human active forces, therefore the transition from the Indian to the Persian periods consisted in passing over from a state of inactivity to one of activity in the material world.

The movement of the hands and everything that was connected with it, the transition from inactivity to physical work is what characterized this epoch. To a much greater degree than is supposed, the inhabitants of ancient India were disinclined to bestir the hands, but in contemplation were much more inclined to lift themselves above the material existence into higher worlds. They had to penetrate deeply into their inner being when they wished to call to memory those earlier states. Therefore the Indian Yoga, for example, consisted in general in giving special care and cultivation to the ether body.

Now let us proceed further. In the culture of the ancient Persian epoch, the ego had sunk into the Soul Body. In that of the Assyrian-Babylonian-Chaldean-Egyptian epoch, the ego mounts into the Sentient Soul. You inquire, what is the Sentient Soul? It is the means by which the sensory human being directs himself outwardly, whereby the perceiving human being by means of his eyes and other senses becomes aware of the ruling spirit in outer nature. Consequently in that epoch, the eyes were directed toward the material things spread out in space, toward the stars and their courses. What was spread out externally in space acted upon the Sentient Soul. In the Egyptian-Chaldean-Assyrian-Babylonian period, very little existed as yet of what can be called an inner, personal and intellectual human culture. We of the present can no longer really imagine what constituted the Egyptian Wisdom of that epoch. It was, in fact, not at all a matter of thinking, a matter of speculation as was the case later on; but when the Egyptian turned his glance toward the outer world, he inwardly experienced the law which he read in the physical world with the physical senses. It was a reading of the laws, a science of perception, a science of feeling, not a science of concepts. If our scholars would only reflect—I am using a harsh expression—then all that has just been said would be pointed out to them, as it were, with fingers, with spiritual fingers. For if the Egyptian did not think with the true, inner forces of the intellect, that means nothing more nor less than that there could not have been, at that time, a real science of thought or of logic. It is true, there was none. History points out to you that the real founder of logic was Aristotle. If there had previously been a logic, a science of thought, it would have been possible to inscribe it in a book. A logic, which is in itself a process of reflection in the ego, in which ideas are united and separated within the ego, in which one forms judgments logically and does not gather them from the things themselves, first appeared in the fourth cultural epoch. Therefore we call this fourth epoch the epoch of the Intellectual Soul, and we ourselves are now in the epoch of the appearance of the ego in the Consciousness Soul. Humanity entered into this epoch about the middle of the Middle Ages, beginning with the 10th, 11th, and 12th Centuries. It came as late as that. The ego first entered the Consciousness Soul about the middle of the Middle Ages.

This can be very easily proven historically, and light could be thrown into every corner were there time to point out much that might come into question. At that time a very definite concept was implanted in mankind, the concept of individual freedom, of individual ego-capacity. If you consider the early part of the Middle Ages, you will still find everywhere that the value of the individual, in a certain sense, depended upon his position in the community. A person inherited his standing, his rank and position from his father and his kinsmen, and in accordance with these impersonal things, which are not consciously connected with the ego, he acted and worked in the world. Only later, when commerce expanded and inventions and modern discoveries were made, did the ego-consciousness begin to extend itself, and we can see arising everywhere in the European world the external reflection of this Consciousness Soul in very definite forms of municipal government, municipal constitution, etc. From the history of this city of Hamburg, for example, it can easily be proven how these things have developed historically. What in the Middle Ages was called the "free city" is the external counterpart of this breathing of the ego-conscious soul through humanity. And if we now allow our glance to sweep into the future, we may say: We are now about to develop this personal consciousness within the Consciousness Soul. All the demands of the modern age are nothing but the demands of the Consciousness Soul which mankind is unconsciously expressing. But when we look still further into the future, we see spiritually something else. The human being then rises in the next cultural epoch, to Manas or Spirit-Self. That will be a time when men will possess a common Wisdom in a very much greater degree than at present; they will be, as it were, immersed in a common Wisdom. This will be the beginning of the feeling that the innermost kernel of the human being is at the same time the most universal. What is looked upon as the possession of the individual, in the present sense of the word, is not yet so on a higher plane. At present there is a notion, closely linked with the individuality, with the human personality, that human beings must contend with one another, must have different opinions. Men say: if we could not have different opinions we would not be independent human beings. Just because they wish to be independent, they must hold different opinions. That, however, is an inferior point of view. Men will be most peaceful and harmonious when they, as separate persons, become most individualized. As long as men are not yet fully overshadowed by Spirit-Self there will be opinions which differ from each other. These opinions are not yet experienced in the true, innermost part of their being. At present there are only a few forerunners of things experienced in the depths of the soul, and these are mathematical and geometrical truths. These cannot be put to the vote. If a million people were to say to you that $2 \times 2 = 5$ and you perceive in your inner being that it is 4, you know that this is true and that the others must be wrong. It is as though someone were to maintain that the sum of the three angles of a triangle does not amount to 180 degrees.

It will be Manas-Culture when more and more the sources of truth are experienced within the strengthened human individuality, within the human personality, and when, at the same time, there is an agreement between what different people experience as higher reality, just as now there is an agreement between what they experience as the truths of mathematics. Men agree upon these mathematical truths at present everywhere, because they are the most elementary truths. In respect of other truths, men contend not because there can be two different right opinions about the same subject, but because they have not yet reached the point of recognizing and fighting down the personal sympathy and antipathy that divides them. Were personal opinions still to come into consideration in simple mathematical truths, many housewives might then, perhaps, agree that $2 \times 2 = 5$ and not 4. For those who see more deeply into the nature of things, it is quite impossible to disagree about their higher nature; there is only one possibility for those who disagree: that of developing themselves to perceive more deeply. Then reality discovered in one soul will coincide exactly with that in another, and there will be no more strife. That is the guarantee for true peace and true brotherhood, because there is but *one* Reality and this Reality has something to do with the Spiritual Sun. Just think how orderly the plants grow; each plant grows toward the sun and there is only a single sun. When in the same way, in the course of the sixth cultural epoch, that Spirit-Self draws into human beings, a Spiritual Sun will actually be present, toward which all men will incline, and in which they will become harmonized. That is the great perspective which we have in prospect for the sixth epoch. Then in the seventh, Life-Spirit or Budhi will, in a certain way, enter into our evolution. This is the far distant future toward which we, only divining, can turn our glance.

But we now see clearly that an epoch will come, the sixth, which will be a very important one; important, because it will bring Peace and Brotherhood through a common Wisdom. Peace and Brotherhood, because not only will the Higher Self sink down into its lower form as Spirit-Self or Manas in certain chosen human beings, but also in that part of humanity passing through a normal evolution. A union of the human ego, as it has been gradually evolved with the higher, the unifying Ego, will then take place. We may call this a spiritual marriage and the union of the human ego with Manas or Spirit-Self was always so called in Esoteric Christianity. However, things of the world are bound closely together and men cannot stretch out their hands, as it were, and draw this Manas or Spirit-Self into themselves. They must reach a very much higher stage of evolution in order to be able to help themselves in respect of these things. In order that the human being in the post-Atlantean age may unite with the Higher Ego, men had to have help in their evolution. When something is to be accomplished, there must be a preparation. If a child is to develop into something special at fifteen years of age, something must be done to that end as early as his sixth or seventh year. Everywhere, evolution must prepare its impulses. What is to happen to mankind in the sixth epoch must be slowly and gradually prepared. The power and force of what is to take place within mankind in the sixth epoch has to come from without.

The first preparation was something still wholly external, operating from the spiritual world, something that had not yet descended into the physical world. That has been pointed out in the great mission of the Hebrew people. When Moses, an Initiate of the Egyptian Mysteries, received those instructions from the Spiritual Guidance of the World which we were able to characterize with the words: "When thou speakest unto them of My laws, tell them that My Name is the 'I AM'," he was charged in these words: "Prepare them by pointing to the formless, invisible God. Point out that, while the Father-God is still active in the blood, the 'I AM' who is to descend even to the physical plane is prepared for those who can understand." This was prepared, as it were, in the third cultural epoch. Out of the Hebrew people we see streaming forth the mission to deliver to humanity the God who then descended deeper into matter and appeared in the flesh. First He was prophesied, then later He appeared to the physical eyes in the flesh. Thus came to expression in the right sense what had been prepared by Moses.

Let us keep this point of time clearly in mind: the spiritual prophecy through Moses, and the conclusion of this prophecy in the appearance of the prophesied Messiah in the Christ. From this time onward—which we can designate as the first division in the history of Christianity—the real Impulse was implanted in human evolution for unity and brotherhood which will eventuate in the sixth epoch. It is like a force that, having sunk down deeply into an object, continues to be active there until gradually results emerge. In a similar way, this spiritual force has been active up to our present time which we must describe as an age in which humanity has wholly descended into matter with all its intellectual and spiritual powers. The question may be asked: Why did Christianity have to come to the world as a direct forerunner of the most deeply materialistic epoch?

Just imagine, for a moment, that humanity had entered into this most deeply materialistic age without Christianity. It would then have been impossible for it to find again the impulse upwards. Think away the Impulse that has been implanted in mankind through the Christ, then the whole of humanity would have had to fall into decadence, would have had to be bound forever to matter. As it is expressed in occultism, it would have been "seized by the force of gravity in matter" and would have been thrown out of its evolution. Thus we must imagine that in the post-Atlantean epoch, mankind made a movement downward into matter, and that before the lowest stage was reached, there came the other Impulse which impelled it again upward in the opposite direction. This was the Christ Impulse. Had the Christ Impulse been active earlier, humanity would never have come to a materialistic development at all. Had it fallen in the ancient Indian epoch, mankind would certainly have been permeated with the spiritual element of Christianity, but it would never have descended deeply enough into matter to have been able to produce all that we call today an outer physical culture. It may seem extraordinary to say that without Christianity there would never have been any railroads, any steamships etc., but for anyone who knows things in their relationship, it is a fact. Never would these means of culture have arisen out of the ancient Indian civilization. There exists a mysterious connection between Christianity and all that is today the so-called pride of mankind. Because Christianity waited until the right moment of time for its appearance, an external culture became possible, and because it entered just at the right moment, it became possible for those who unite themselves with the Christ Principle to be able to rise again out of materiality. However, since Christianity has been received without understanding, it has become very greatly materialized. Because it has been so greatly misunderstood, it has itself been materialistically interpreted. Thus, in a certain way, it is a very distorted, materialistic form which Christianity has assumed in the course of that period which we have just been following right up to our own times, and which we may designate as a second division of Christian history. Instead of the Last Supper, for example, being apprehended from its higher spiritual aspect, it has become materialized and has been represented as a transubstantiation of gross physical substance. And we could instance hundreds and hundreds of examples of the fact that Christianity as a spiritual phenomenon has not been understood.

We have now almost reached the moment when this second period ends, when men must of necessity form a connection with the spiritual aspect of Christianity, with what Christianity really should be, in order that its true spiritual content may be drawn forth. This will come about through the Anthroposophic deepening of Christianity. By applying Anthroposophy to Christianity, we are following the universal historic necessity of preparing the third Christian epoch which directs its life toward the in-streaming of Manas in the sixth epoch. That will be, as it were, the third chapter. The first chapter is the period of the prediction of Christianity up to the time of the appearance of Christ Jesus and a little beyond. The second chapter is the deepest possible immersion of the human spirit in matter and the materialization of Christianity itself. The third chapter will be a spiritual understanding of Christianity by means of a deepening of the soul through Anthroposophy. That such a document as the Gospel of St. John has not, up to our own age, been understood is due to our whole materialistic evolution. Such a materialistic culture as has gradually developed could not fully understand this Gospel. The spiritual culture which must begin with the Anthroposophic Movement will understand this document in its truly spiritual form and prepare what will then lead over into the sixth epoch.

For those who have attained a Christian or a Rosicrucian initiation—even for those who have attained any initiation whatsoever—an extraordinary phenomenon makes its appearance. Things which take place acquire for them a double meaning; one which is enacted in the outer physical world, another, by means of which things enacted in the physical world become indications of great, comprehensive spiritual happenings. You will, therefore, understand if I now attempt to describe somewhat the impressions of the writer of the Gospel of St. John on one particular occasion.

An extraordinary event took place during the life of Christ Jesus and this event occurred upon the physical plane. The one who is describing it, according to the Gospel, does so as an initiate. Accordingly, the event represents to him simultaneously the perceptions and the results that accrue during the process of initiation. Picture to yourselves the end of this act of initiation.

During three and a half time periods, which in ancient times, as we have already pointed out, were represented by three and a half days, the candidate for initiation lay in a lethargic sleep. Each day he experienced something different in respect of the spiritual world. On the first day he had definite experiences which presented to him events in the spiritual worlds; and on the two subsequent days he had still other experiences. Now in this particular passage of the Gospel, the person we are considering had shown to him what is always spiritually presented to the clairvoyant faculty, that is, the future of mankind. If we know the impulses of the future, we can then inject them into the present and thereby lead the present over into the future.

Picture to yourselves the seer of that age. He experienced the spiritual meaning of the first of the three chapters I have described from the time when the command resounded: "Say unto your people, I am the 'I AM',", to the descent of the Messiah. As second chapter he experienced the descent of the Christ into matter, and as third chapter he experienced how gradually mankind is being prepared to receive the Spirit or Spirit-Self (Manas) in the sixth epoch. He experienced all this in an astral pre-vision. He experienced the marriage of humanity with the Spirit. That is an important experience which mankind can only impress upon the outer world through Christ having entered into *time*, into history. Previously mankind had not lived in this kind of brotherliness, brought about by means of the spirit unfolding within the inner being, in which peace

exists between man and man. Prior to this, there was only the love prepared physically through the tie of blood. This love develops gradually
into a spiritual love which then descends upon earth. As final result
of this third chapter of initiation, we may say that humanity celebrates
its marriage with Spirit-Self or Manas. This can only happen when the
time for it has arrived, when the time has matured for the full realization of the Christ Impulse. So long as the time has not yet come, so long
will the relationship which is based upon the kinship of blood obtain, and
so long will love be an un-spiritual form of love.

Wherever in ancient documents numbers are mentioned, the hidden
aspect of numbers is meant. When we read, "On the third day there was
a marriage in Cana of Galilee," every initiate knows that with this "third
day," something very special is meant. What is meant? The writer of
the Gospel of St. John points out that it is not alone a matter of an
actual experience, but that it is, at the same time, a great, an overpowering
prophecy. This marriage expresses the great marriage of humanity which
occurred on the third day of initiation. On the first day there occurred
what took place in the transition from the third to the fourth cultural
epoch; on the second day, what took place in the transition from the
fourth to the fifth epoch and on the third day what will occur when
mankind passes over from the fifth to the sixth epoch. These are the three
days of initiation. The Christ Impulse has been compelled to wait until
the third epoch. Before that, the time had not come when it could operate.
The Gospel of St. John points to a special relationship between "me and
thee," between "us two." That is what is really said, not the absurd
"Woman, what have I to do with thee." When the Mother asks the Christ
to make a sign, He answered: "My time is not yet come" to be active
at marriages, that is, to bring people together. That time is yet to come.
What is based upon the blood-bond still works on and will continue to be
active; hence the reference to the relationship between mother and son at
the Marriage of Cana.

When we consider the documents in this way, all that is really external stands out in bold relief against a significant spiritual background.
We gaze into the abysmal depths of the spiritual life when we penetrate
into what has been bestowed upon mankind by such an initiate as the
writer of the Gospel of St. John, into what he was able to bestow upon it,

because the Christ had implanted His Impulse within human evolution.

Therefore we have seen that these things must be explained by the astral reality which the initiate experiences, not by empty allegory or symbolism. We are not dealing with a symbolic interpretation only, but with the narration of the experiences of the initiate. If this were not so, then one might feel that those who stand outside are right when they say that Spiritual Science offers nothing but allegorical interpretations. If we apply to this passage the spiritual-scientific interpretation, as we now understand it, we learn how, through three cosmic days, the Christ Impulse works upon humanity, from the third cultural epoch over into the fourth, from the fourth to the fifth and from the fifth into the sixth. And viewing this evolution from the standpoint of the Gospel of St. John, we are now able to say: The Christ Impulse was so great that mankind of the present has understood but very little of it, and only in a later age will it be wholly comprehended.

XI

CHRISTIAN INITIATION

If in this whole lecture course we are to concentrate our efforts on gaining a deeper understanding of the words "Father and Mother of Jesus," and consequently of the essence of Christianity in general according to the Gospel of St. John, we must first acquire the material for an understanding of the concept, Mother and Father, in its spiritual sense, as it is intended in this Gospel and at the same time in its actual meaning. For it is not a question of an allegorical or a symbolic explanation.

We must first understand what it means to unite oneself with the higher spiritual worlds, to prepare oneself to receive the higher worlds. We must at the same time consider the nature of initiation, especially in regard to the Gospel of St. John. Let us ask: What is an initiate?

In all ages of the post-Atlantean human evolution, an initiate has been a person who could lift himself above the outer physical sense-world and have his own personal experiences in the spiritual worlds, a person who could experience the spiritual worlds just as the ordinary human being experiences the physical sense-world through the outer senses, eyes, ears, etc. Such an initiate becomes then a witness of those worlds and their truths. That is one aspect. But there is also something else very essential which every initiate acquires as a very special characteristic during his initiation, that is, he lifts himself above the feelings and sensations which are not only justified but also very necessary within the physical world, but which cannot, however, exist in the same way in the spiritual world.

Do not misunderstand what is said here and imagine that anyone who is able, as an initiate, to experience the spiritual world as well as the physical world must give up all other human feelings and sensations which are of value here in the physical world and exchange them for those of the higher worlds. This is not so. He does not exchange one for the other, but he acquires one in addition to the other. If, on the one hand, he has to spiritualize his feelings, he must, on the other, strengthen much more those feelings which are of use for working in the physical world. In this way we must interpret those words used in connection

with an initiate, namely, that he must, in a certain sense, become a homeless person. It is not meant that in any sense he must become estranged
from his home and his family as long as he lives in the physical world,
but these words have at least this much significance, that by acquiring
the corresponding feelings in the spiritual world, the feelings for the physical world will experience a finer, more beautiful development. What
does it mean to be homeless? It means that one without this designation
cannot, in the true sense of the word, attain initiation. To be a homeless
man, means that he must develop no special sympathies in the spiritual
world similar to those he possesses here in the physical world for special
regions or relationships. The individual human being in the physical
world belongs to some particular folk or to some particular family, to
this or that community of the state. That is all quite proper. He does
not need to lose this; he needs it here. If, however, he wished to employ
these feelings in the spiritual world, he would bring a very bad dowry
to that world. There, it is not a question of developing sympathy for
anything, but of allowing everything to work upon him objectively,
according to its inherent worth. It could also be said, were this generally
understood, that an initiate must be, in the fullest sense of the word, an
objective human being.

It is just through its evolution upon the earth that humanity has
emerged out of a former homeless state connected with the ancient
dreamy, clairvoyant consciousness. We have seen how mankind has
descended out of the spiritual spheres into the physical world. In the
primal spiritual spheres, patriotism and such things did not exist. When
humanity descended from the spiritual spheres, one part peopled the
earth in one region and another part in another region, and thus the
individual groups of human beings of different regions became stereotype
copies of those regions. Do not imagine that the negro became black
solely from inner reasons; he became black also through adapting himself
to the region of the earth in which he lived. And so it was also with the
white people. Just as the great differences of colour and race came into
existence because human beings have acquired something through their
connection with their environment, so is it also true in respect of the
smaller differences in folk individuality. But this has again to do with
the specialization of love upon the earth. Because men became dissimilar,

love was at first established in small communities. Only gradually will humanity be able to evolve out of the small communities into a large community of love which will develop concretely through the very implanting of the Spirit-Self. The initiate had to anticipate whither human evolution is tending in order to overcome and bridge over all barriers and bring about great peace, great harmony and brotherhood. In his homelessness, he must always, at the very beginning, receive the same rudiments of great brotherly love. This was symbolically expressed in ancient times in the descriptions of the wanderings experienced by the initiate, such as those, for example, of Pythagoras. Why was this described? In order that the initiate might become objective toward every thing in the feelings he had developed within the heart of the community. It is the task of Christianity to bring to the whole of humanity the Impulse of this Brotherhood which the initiate always possessed as an *individual* impulse.

Let us hold clearly in mind that most profound idea of Christianity, that the Christ is the Spirit of the earth and that the earth is His body or vesture. And let us take it literally, for we have said that we must weigh in the balance each separate word of such a document as the Gospel of St. John. What do we learn with respect to the "vesture of the earth" when we make a survey of evolution? We learn, first of all, the fact that the vesture of the earth—that is, the solid parts of it—was divided. One person took possession of this part, another of that part. This part belonged to one person, that part to another. Possession, i.e. the extension of the personality through the acquisition of property, is in a certain sense that into which the garment worn by the Christ, the Spirit of the earth, has, in the course of time, been divided. One thing alone could not be divided, but belonged to all; this was the airy envelope surrounding the earth. And from this airy covering, the breath of life was breathed into the human being, as we are shown in the myths of Paradise. Here we have the first rudiments of the ego in the physical body. The air cannot be divided. Let us try to find out whether the one who described Christianity most profoundly in the Gospel of St. John has anywhere indicated this:

And they parted His garments; but His coat they did not divide.

Here you have the words which give you an explanation of how the earth as a whole, together with its airy envelope, is the body or garment, and the coat of the Christ. The garments of the Christ were divided into continents and regions; but not the coat. The air has not been divided; it remains a common possession of all. It is the external, material symbol for the love which is hovering about the earthly globe, which will later be realized.

And in many other connections, Christianity must bring mankind to an acceptance of some of the ancient principles of initiation. If we wish to understand this, we must now characterize initiation. It will suffice, if we consider especially the three main types of initiation; the ancient Yoga, the really specific Christian initiation, and that initiation which is entirely appropriate for men of the present day, the Christian-Rosicrucian initiation. We intend now to describe what course initiation, in general, takes in all three of these forms; what it is and what it represents.

How does a human being become capable of perception in spiritual worlds? First, let me ask, how have you become capable of observing in the physical world? The physical body has sense-organs that make this possible. If you trace human evolution very far back, you will find that in primeval times, the human creature did not yet possess eyes for seeing and ears for hearing in the physical world, but that, as Goethe says, all organs were still undifferentiated. As proof of this, just recall how certain lower animals today still have these undifferentiated organs. Certain lower animals have points through which they can distinguish only light and darkness, and out of these undifferentiated organs, eyes and ears have been moulded and formed. They have been worked into the plastic substance of the physical body. Because your eye has been moulded, there exists for you a world of colour, and because your ear has been sculptured, a world of tone is audible to you. No one has the right to say that a world does not really exist; he may only say, "I do not perceive it." For to see the world in the true sense of the word, means that I have the organs with which to perceive it. One may say: "I know only this or that world," but one may not say: "I do not admit of the existence of a world that someone else perceives." A person who speaks in this manner demands that others too should perceive only just what he himself perceives, but nothing else; he claims authoritatively that only what he perceives is true. When at present someone appears and says: "That is all Anthroposophical imagining, what Anthroposophists declare exists, does not exist," he only proves that he and those like him do not perceive these worlds. We take the positive standpoint. Whoever grants only the existence of what he himself perceives, demands not only that we acknowledge what he knows, but he wishes to make an authoritative decision about something of which he knows nothing. There is no greater intolerance than that shown by official science toward Spiritual Science, and it will become even worse than it has ever been before! It appears in the most varied forms. People are not at all conscious of saying something which they should not allow themselves to say. In many gatherings of very good Christians, one can hear it said: "Anthroposophists talk of some kind of an esoteric Christian teaching, but Christianity needs no esoteric teaching; for only that can be true which a simple, unpretentious mind can perceive and understand," which means, of course, only what the speaker can perceive and understand. He therefore requires that no one should perceive and understand anything different from what he himself perceives and understands. The infallibility of the Pope is quite properly not acknowledged in such Christian assemblies, but the infallibility of the individual is claimed today in the widest circles even by the Christians. Anthroposophy is attacked as a result of this papal standpoint in consequence of which each individual sets himself up as a kind of little pope.

If we consider that the physical sense-world exists for us because the individual organs have been carved into the physical body, it will no longer seem extraordinary when it is said that perception in a higher world rests upon the fact that higher organs have been formed in the higher members of the human organism, in the ether and astral bodies. The physical body is, in this way, already provided with its sense-organs, but the ether and astral bodies are not yet so provided; these have still to be carved into them. When this has been done, there exists what is called perception in the higher worlds.

We shall now speak of the way in which these organs are built into the ether and astral bodies. We have said that in anyone who aspires to initiation and has attained it, higher organs have been developed. How is this accomplished? It is a matter of understanding the human astral body in the state in which it exists in its purity. During the day this astral body is immersed in the physical body. There the forces of the physical body act upon it; it is not then free. It carries out the demands of the physical body; hence it is impossible to begin the development of these higher organs during the day. It can be begun when the astral body is out of the physical body, in sleep; only then can the astral body be moulded. The human astral body can only have its higher sense organs developed when they are carved into it during sleep, while outside the physical body. But we cannot manipulate a sleeping human being; that would not be possible for the modern man, if he wishes to perceive what is happening to him in sleep. If you have him in an unconscious condition, then he cannot observe this. Here there seems to be a contradiction, for the astral body is not conscious of its connection with the physical body during sleep. But *indirectly* it is possible that during the day the physical body is acted upon and the impressions which it then receives remain within the astral body when this is withdrawn at night. Just as the impressions which the astral body receives from the surrounding physical world have been impressed upon it, so in like manner we must do something quite specific with the physical body, in order that this something be imprinted upon the astral body and then be formed in it in the proper manner. This happens when the human being ceases to live in his customary way during the day, allowing random impressions to enter his consciousness, and takes his inner life in hand by means of a methodical schooling in the manner described. This is called Meditation, Concentration or Contemplation. These are exercises which are as strictly prescribed in the schools for the purpose, as microscopy is prescribed in the laboratories. If a person carries out these exercises, they act so intensely upon him that the astral body is plastically re-shaped when it withdraws during sleep. Just as this sponge adapts itself to the form of my hand as long as I hold it there, but forms itself again according to the forces inherent in it as soon as I release it, so in like manner is it with the astral body; when in sleep it withdraws from the corporality, it follows the astral forces invested in it. Thus it is during the day that we must undertake those spiritual activities by means of which the astral body, during the night, is plastically formed so that organs of higher perception are developed in it.

Meditation can be regulated in a threefold manner. 1. There can be more consideration given to the thought-matter, to the so-called elements of Wisdom, the pure element of thought. This is the Yoga training which deals especially with the element of thought, Contemplation. 2. One can work more upon the feeling through its special cultivation. This is the specifically Christian course. 3. Again one can work through a combination of feeling and will. This is the Christian-Rosicrucian method. To consider the Yoga practice would carry us too far, and it would also have no relationship to the Gospel of St. John. We shall consider the specifically Christian initiation and explain its basis. You must think of this form of initiation as one which a person belonging to the present social order could hardly undergo. It demands a temporary isolation. The Rosicrucian method, however, is the method by which we can work ourselves into the higher worlds without interfering with our duties. What, however, is applicable in principle, we can also fully explain by means of Christian initiation.

This method of initiation has to do exclusively with the feelings, and I shall now have to enumerate seven experiences of the feeling-life; seven stages of feeling, through the experiencing of which the astral body is actually so affected that it develops its organs during the night. Let us describe how the Christian neophyte must live in order that he may pass through these stages. The first stage is what is called "Washing the Feet." Here the teacher says to the pupil: "Observe the plants. They have their roots in the ground; the mineral earth is a lower being than the plant. If the plant were able to contemplate its own nature, it would have to say to the earth; it is true I am a higher being, but if thou wert not there, I could not exist; for from thee, O earth, I draw most of my sustenance. If the plant were able to translate this into feeling, it would then bow itself down to the stone and say:—I bow myself before thee, O stone, thou humbler being, for I am indebted to thee for my very existence! Then if we ascend to the animal, it would have to behave in a similar manner toward the plant and say: Indeed it is true, I am higher than the plant, but to the lower kingdoms I owe my existence! If in this manner we mount higher and reach the human being, then each individual who stands somewhat higher in the social scale must incline himself to the lower and say: To those on the lower social level I owe my existence! This continues on up to Christ-Jesus. The Twelve who are about Him are at a level lower than Christ-Jesus; but as the plant develops out of the stone, so does the Christ grow out of the Twelve. He bows down to the Twelve and says: I owe you My existence."

When the teacher had explained this to the pupil, he then said to him: "For weeks must thou surrender thyself to this cosmic feeling of how the superior should incline to the inferior and when thou hast thoroughly developed this feeling within thee, then wilt thou experience an inner and an outer symptom!" These are not the essential things, they only indicate that the pupil has practiced sufficiently. When the physical body was sufficiently influenced by the soul, this was indicated to him by an external symptom in which he feels as though water were lapping over his feet. That is a very real feeling! And he has another very real feeling in which the "Washing of the Feet" appears to him as in a mighty vision in the astral, the inclining of the Higher Self to the lower. Thus the occult student experiences in the astral world what is found depicted in the Gospel of St. John as an historical fact.

At the second stage, the pupil is told: "Thou must develop within thyself yet another feeling. Thou must picture how it would be were all the suffering and sorrow possible in the world to come upon thee; thou must feel how it would be wert thou exposed to the piling up of all possible hindrances, and thou must enter into the feeling that thou must stand erect even though all the adversity of the world were to bear down upon thee!" Then when the pupil has practised this exercise for a sufficient length of time, there are again two symptoms; in the first he has the feeling of being beaten from all sides, and in the second he has an astral vision of the "Scourging." I am relating what hundreds of people have experienced whereby they have acquired the ability to mount into the higher worlds.

In the third exercise, the pupil had to imagine that the holiest thing that he possesses, which he defends with his whole ego-being, is subjected to jeers and gibes. He must say to himself:—"Come what may, I must hold myself erect and defend what is holy to me." When he had accustomed himself to this, he felt something like pricking upon his head, and he experienced the "Crown of Thorns" as an astral vision. Again it must be said that the important thing is not the symptoms; they appear as a result of the exercises. Care was also taken that there was no question of suggestion and auto-suggestion.

In the fourth exercise, the pupil's body must become as foreign to his feelings as any external object—a stick of wood for example—and he must not say "I" to his body. This experience must become so much a part of his feelings that he says: "I carry my body about with me as I do my coat." He connects his ego no longer with his body. Then something occurs which is called the Stigmata. What in many cases might be a condition of sickness is in this case a result of Meditation, because all sickness must be eliminated. On the feet and hands and on the right side of the breast appear the so-called Stigmata; and as an inner symptom, he beholds the "Crucifixion" in an astral vision.

The fifth, sixth and seventh grades of feeling, we can only briefly describe. The fifth grade consists of what is called "The Mystical Death." Through feelings which the pupil is permitted to experience at this stage, he feels as though, in an instant, a black curtain were drawn before the whole physical, visible world and as though everything had disappeared. This moment is important because of something else that must be experienced, if one wishes to push on into Christian initiation, in the true sense of the word. The pupil then feels that he can plunge into the primal causes of evil, pain, affliction and sorrow. And he can suffer all the evil that exists in the depths of the human soul, when he descends into Hell. That is the "Descent into Hell." When this has been experienced, it is as though the black curtain had been rent asunder and he looks into the spiritual world.

The sixth step is what is called the "Interment and Resurrection." This is the stage at which the pupil feels himself one with the entire earthbody. He feels as though he were laid within and belonged to the whole earth planet. His life has been extended into a planetary existence.

The seventh experience cannot be described in words; only one could describe it who is able to think without the physical brain instrument—and for that there is no language, because our language has only designations for the physical plane. Therefore, only a reference can be made to this stage. It surpasses anything that the human being can possibly conceive. This is called the "Ascension" or the complete absorption into the spiritual world.

This completes the gamut of feelings into which the pupil, during waking day-consciousness, must place himself with complete inner equanimity. When the pupil has surrendered himself to these experiences, they act so strongly upon the astral body that, in the night, inner sense-organs are developed, are plastically formed. These seven steps of feeling are not practiced in the Rosicrucian initiation, but the result is the same as that of which we have just spoken.

Thus you see that the important thing in initiation is to influence the astral body in such a way by the indirect means of the day-experiences, that it may, when it is wholly free during the night, take on a new plastic form. When the human being in this manner, as an astral being, has given himself a plastic form, the astral body has become actually a new member of the human organism. He is then wholly permeated by Manas or Spirit-Self.

When the astral body is thus divided, that part which has in this way been plastically formed is brought over into the ether body. And just as you press the seal upon the sealing-wax, and the name on the seal appears not only on the seal, but on the wax as well, so too must the astral body dip down into the ether body and impress upon it whatever it may now possess. The inner process, the working over of the astral body, is the same in all methods of initiation. Only in the method of transmission into the ether body do the individual methods differ. We shall speak tomorrow of these differences and show how the three methods of initiation, which have proved to be the most profound evolutionary impulses in the course of the post-Atlantean age, differ from each other and what significance initiation, in general, has for human evolution. Then these parts of the Gospel of St. John upon which we have not yet been able to touch will also become clear.

XII

THE NATURE OF THE VIRGIN SOPHIA
AND OF THE HOLY SPIRIT

Yesterday we reached the point of discussing the change which takes place in the human astral body through Meditation, Concentration and other practices which are given in the various methods of initiation. We have seen that the astral body is thereby affected in such a way that it develops within itself the organs which it needs for perceiving in the higher worlds and we have said that up to this point, the principle of initiation is everywhere really the same—although the forms of its practices conform wholly to the respective cultural epochs. The principal difference appears with the occurrence of the next thing which must follow. In order that the pupil may be able actually to perceive in the higher worlds, it is necessary that the organs which have been formed out of the astral part, impress or stamp themselves upon the ether body, be impressed into the etheric element.

The re-fashioning of the astral body indirectly through Meditation and Concentration, is called by an ancient name, "katharsis," or purification. Katharsis or purification has as its purpose the discarding from the astral body all that hinders it from becoming harmoniously and regularly organized, thus enabling it to acquire higher organs. It is endowed with the germ of these higher organs; it is only necessary to bring forth the forces which are present in it. We have said that the most varied methods can be employed for bringing about this katharsis. A person can go very far in this matter of katharsis if, for example, he has gone through and inwardly experienced all that is in my book, *Philosophy of Spiritual Activity,* and feels that this book was for him a stimulation and that now he has reached the point where he can himself actually reproduce the thoughts just as they are there presented. If a person holds the same relationship to this book that a virtuoso, in playing a selection on the piano, holds to the composer of the piece, that is, he reproduces the whole thing within himself—naturally according to his ability to do so—then through the strictly built up sequence of thought of this book—for it is written in this manner—katharsis will be developed to a high degree. For the important point in such things as this book is that the thoughts are all placed in such a way that they become active. In many other books of the present, just by changing the system a little, what has been said earlier in the book can just as well be said later. In the *Philosophy of Spiritual Activity* this is not possible. Page 150 can as little be placed fifty pages earlier in the subject matter as the hind legs of a dog can be exchanged with the forelegs, for the book is a logically arranged organism and the working out of the thoughts in it has an effect similar to an inner schooling. Hence there are various methods of bringing about katharsis. If a person has not been successful in doing this after having gone through this book, he should not think that what has been said is untrue, but rather that he has not studied it properly or with sufficient energy or thoroughness.

Something else must now be considered and that is that when this katharsis has taken place, when the astral organs have been formed in the astral body, it must all be imprinted upon the ether body. In the pre-Christian initiation, it was done in the following manner. After the pupil had undergone the suitable preparatory training, which often lasted for years, he was told: The time has now come when the astral body has developed far enough to have astral organs of perception, now these can become aware of their counterpart in the ether body. Then the pupil was subjected to a procedure which today—at least for our cultural epoch—is not only unnecessary, but is not in all seriousness feasible. He was put into a lethargic condition for three and a half days, and was treated during this time in such a way that not only the astral body left the physical and ether bodies—a thing that occurs every night in sleep—but to a certain degree the ether body also was lifted out; but care was taken that the physical body remained intact and that the pupil did not die in the meantime. The ether body was then liberated from the forces of the physical body which act upon it. It had become, as it were, elastic and plastic and when the sensory organs that had been formed in the astral body sank down into it, the ether body received an imprint from the whole astral body. When the pupil was brought again into a normal condition by the Hierophant, when the astral body and ego were again united with the physical and ether bodies—a procedure which the Hierophant well understood—then not only did he experience katharsis, but also what is called "Illumination" or "Photismos." The pupil could then not only perceive in the world around him all those things that were physically perceptible, but he could employ the spiritual organs of perception, which means, he could see and perceive the spiritual. Initiation consisted essentially of these two processes, Purification or Purging, and Illumination.

Then the course of human evolution entered upon a phase in which it gradually became impossible to draw the ether body out of the physical without a very great disturbance in all its functions, because the whole tendency of the post-Atlantean evolution was to cause the ether body to be attached closer and closer to the physical body. It was consequently necessary to carry out other methods of initiation which proceed in such a manner that without the separating of the physical and ether bodies, the astral body, having become sufficiently developed through katharsis and able of itself to return again to the physical and etheric bodies, was able to imprint its organs on the ether body in spite of the hindrance of the physical body. What had to happen was that stronger forces had to become active in Meditation and Concentration in order that there might be the strong impulse in the astral body for overcoming the power of resistance of the physical body. In the first place there was the actual specifically Christian initiation in which it was necessary for the pupil to undergo the procedure which was described yesterday as the seven steps. When he had undergone these feelings and experiences, his astral body had been so intensely affected it formed its organs of perception plastically —perhaps only after years, but still sooner or later—and then impressed them upon the ether body, thus making of the pupil one of the Illuminati. This kind of initiation which is specifically Christian could only be described fully, if I were able to hold lectures about its particular aspects, every day for about a fortnight instead of only for a few days. But that is not the important thing. Yesterday you were given certain details of the Christian initiation. We only wish to become acquainted with its principle.

By continually meditating upon passages of the Gospel of St. John, the Christian pupil is actually in a condition to reach initiation without the three and a half day continued lethargic sleep. If each day he allows the first verses of the Gospel of St. John, from "In the beginning was the Word" to the passage "full of devotion and truth," to work upon him, they become an exceedingly significant meditation. They have this force within them, for this Gospel is not there simply to be read and understood in its entirety with the intellect, but it must be inwardly fully experienced and felt. It is a force which comes to the help of initiation and works for it. Then will the "Washing of the Feet," the "Scourging" and other inner processes be experienced as astral visions, wholly corresponding to the description in the Gospel itself, beginning with the 13th Chapter.

The Rosicrucian initiation, although resting upon a Christian foundation works more with other symbolic ideas which produce katharsis, chiefly with imaginative pictures. That is another modification which had to be used, because mankind had progressed a step further in its evolution and the methods of initiation must conform to what has gradually been evolved.

We must understand that when a person has attained this initiation, he is fundamentally quite different from the person he was before it. While formerly he was only associated with the things of the physical world, he now acquires the possibility likewise of association with the events and beings of the spiritual world. This pre-supposes that the human being acquires knowledge in a much more real sense than in that abstract, dry, prosaic sense in which we usually speak of knowledge. For a person who acquires spiritual knowledge, finds the process to be something quite different. It is a complete realization of that beautiful expression, "Know thyself." But the most dangerous thing in the realm of knowledge is to grasp these words erroneously and today this occurs only too frequently. Many people construe these words to mean that they should no longer look about the physical world, but should gaze into their own inner being and seek there for everything spiritual. This is a very mistaken understanding of the saying, for that is not at all what it means. We must clearly understand that true higher knowledge is also an evolution from one standpoint, which the human being has attained, to another which he had not reached previously. If a person practices self-knowledge only by brooding upon himself, he sees only what he already possesses. He thereby acquires nothing new, but only knowledge of his own lower self in the present meaning of the word. This inner nature is only one part that is necessary for knowledge. The other part that is necessary must be added. Without the two parts, there is no real knowledge. By means of his inner nature, he can develop organs through which he can gain knowledge. But just as the eye, as an external sense organ, would not perceive the sun by gazing into itself, but only by looking outward at the sun, so must the inner perceptive organs gaze outwardly, in other words, gaze into an *external spiritual* in order actually to perceive. The concept "Knowledge" had a much deeper, a more real meaning in those ages when spiritual things were better understood than at present. Read in the Bible the words, "Abraham knew his wife!" or this or that Patriarch "knew his wife". One does not need to seek very far in order to understand that by this expression fructification is meant. When one considers the words, "Know thyself," in the Greek, they do not mean that you stare into your own inner being, but that you fructify yourself with what streams into you from the spiritual world. "Know thyself" means: Fructify thyself with the content of the spiritual world!

Two things are needed for this namely, that the human being prepare himself through katharsis and illumination, and then that he open his inner being freely to the spiritual world. In this connection we may liken his inner nature to the female aspect, the outer spiritual to the male. The inner being must be made susceptible of receiving the higher self. When this has happened, then the higher human self streams into him from the spiritual world. One may ask: Where is this higher human self? Is it within the personal man? No, it is not there. On Saturn, Sun and Moon, the higher self was diffused over the entire cosmos. At that time the Cosmic Ego was spread out over all human kind, but now men have to permit it to work upon them. They must permit this Ego to work upon their previously prepared inner natures. This means that the human inner nature, in other words, the astral body has to be cleansed, purified and ennobled and subjected to katharsis, then a person may expect that the external spirit will stream into him for his illumination. That will occur when the human being has been so well prepared that he has subjected his astral body to katharsis, thereby developing his inner organs of perception. The astral body, in any case, has progressed so far that now when it dips down into the ether and physical bodies, illumination or photismos results. What actually occurs is that the astral body imprints its organs upon the ether body, making it possible for the human being to perceive a spiritual world about him; making it possible for his inner being, the astral body, to receive what the ether body is able to offer to it, what the ether body draws out of the entire cosmos, out of the Cosmic Ego.

This cleansed, purified astral body, which bears within it at the moment of illumination none of the impure impressions of the physical world, but only the organs of perception of the spiritual world is called in esoteric Christianity the "pure, chaste, wise Virgin Sophia." By means of all that he receives during katharsis, the pupil cleanses and purifies his astral body so that it is transformed into the Virgin Sophia. And when the Virgin Sophia encounters the Cosmic Ego, the Universal Ego which causes illumination, the pupil is surrounded by light, spiritual light. This second power that approaches the Virgin Sophia, is called in esoteric Christianity—is also so called today—the "Holy Spirit." Therefore according to esoteric Christianity, it is correct to say that through his processes of initiation the Christian esotericist attains the purification and cleansing of his astral body; he makes his astral body into the Virgin Sophia and is illuminated from above—if you wish, you may call it overshadowed—by the "Holy Spirit," by the Cosmic, Universal Ego. And a person thus illuminated, who, in other words, according to esoteric Christianity has received the "Holy Spirit" into himself, speaks forthwith in a different manner. How does he speak? When he speaks about Saturn, Sun and Moon, about the different members of the human being, about the processes of cosmic evolution, he is not expressing *his* own opinion. *His* views do not at all come into consideration. When such a person speaks about Saturn, it is Saturn itself that is speaking through him. When he speaks about the Sun, the Spiritual Being of the Sun speaks through him. He is the instrument. His personal ego has been eclipsed, which means that at such moments it has become impersonal and it is the Cosmic Universal Ego that is using his ego as its instrument through which to speak. Therefore, in true esoteric teaching which proceeds from esoteric Christianity, one should not speak of *views* or *opinions,* for in the highest sense of the word this is incorrect; there are no such things. According to esoteric Christianity, whoever speaks with the right attitude of mind toward the world will say to himself, for instance: If I tell people that there were two horses outside, the important thing is not that one of them pleases me less than the other and that I think one is a worthless horse. The important point is that I describe the horses to the others and give the facts. In like manner, what has been observed in the spiritual worlds must be described irrespective of all personal opinions. In every spiritual-scientific system of teaching, only the series of facts must be related and this must have nothing to do with the opinions of the one who relates them.

Thus we have acquired two concepts in their spiritual significance. We have learned to know the nature of the Virgin Sophia, which is the purified astral body, and the nature of the "Holy Spirit," the Cosmic Universal Ego, which is received by the Virgin Sophia and which can then speak out of this purified astral body. There is something else to be attained, a still higher stage, that is the ability to help someone else, the ability to give him the impulse to accomplish both of these. Men of our evolutionary epoch can receive the Virgin Sophia (the purified astral body) and the Holy Spirit (illumination) in the manner described, but only Christ Jesus could give to the earth what was necessary to accomplish this. He has implanted in the spiritual part of the earth those forces which make it possible for that to happen at all which has been described in the Christian initiation. You may ask how did this come about?

Two things are necessary for an understanding of this. First we must make ourselves acquainted with something purely historical, that is, with the manner of giving of names which was quite different in the age in which the Gospels were written from the way in which it is done at present.

Those who interpret the Gospel at present do not at all understand the principle of giving names at the time the Gospels were written and therefore they do not speak as they should. It is, in fact, exceedingly difficult to describe the principle of giving names at that time, yet we can make it comprehensible, even though we only indicate it in rough outlines. Let us suppose, in the case of someone whom we meet, that instead of holding to the name which does not at all fit him, and which has been given to him in the abstract way customary today, we were to harken to and notice his most distinguishing characteristics, were to notice the most prominent attribute of his character and were in a position to discern clairvoyantly the deeper foundations of his being, then were to give him his name in accordance with those most important qualities which we believe should be attributed to him. Were we to follow such a method of giving names, we should be doing something, at a lower more elementary stage, similar to what was done at that time by those who gave names in the manner of the writer of the Gospel of St. John. In order to make very clear his manner of giving names, let us consider the following:

The author of the St. John's Gospel regarded the physical, historic Mother of Jesus in her most prominent characteristics and asked himself,—Where shall I find a name for her which will express most perfectly her real being? Then, because she had, by means of her earlier incarnations, reached those spiritual heights upon which she stood; and because she appeared in her external personality to be a counterpart, a revelation of what was called in esoteric Christianity, the Virgin Sophia, he called the Mother of Jesus the "Virgin Sophia;" and this is what she was always called in the esoteric places where esoteric Christianity was taught. Exoterically he leaves her entirely un-named in contradistinction to those others who have chosen for her the secular name, Mary. He could not take the secular name, he had to express in the name the profound, world historic evolution. He does this by indicating that she cannot be called Mary and what is more, he places by her side her sister Mary, wife of Cleophas and calls her simply the "Mother of Jesus." He shows thereby that he does not wish to mention her name, that it cannot be publicly revealed. In esoteric circles, she is always called the "Virgin Sophia." It was she who represented the "Virgin Sophia" as an external historical personality.

If we now wish to penetrate further into the nature of Christianity and its founder, we must take under consideration yet another mystery. We should understand clearly how to make a distinction between the personality who, in Esoteric Christianity, was called "Jesus of Nazareth" and Him who was called "Christ Jesus," the Christ dwelling within Jesus of Nazareth.

Now what does this mean? It means that in the historical personality of Jesus of Nazareth, we have to do with a highly developed human being who had passed through many incarnations and after a cycle of high development was again reincarnated; a person who, because of this, was attracted to a mother so pure that the writer of the Gospel could call her the "Virgin Sophia." Thus we are dealing with a highly developed human being, Jesus of Nazareth, who had progressed far in his evolution in his previous incarnations and in this incarnation had entered upon a highly spiritual stage. The other evangelists were not illuminated to such a high degree as the writer of this Gospel. It was more the actual sense-world that was revealed to them, a world in which they saw their Master and Messiah moving about as Jesus of Nazareth. The mysterious spiritual relationships, at least those of the heights into which the writer of the Gospel of St. John could peer, were concealed from them. For this reason they laid special emphasis upon the fact that in Jesus of Nazareth lived the Father, who had always existed in Judaism and was transmitted down through the generations as the God of the Jews. And they expressed this when they said: "If we trace back the ancestry of Jesus of Nazareth through generation after generation, we are able to prove that the same blood flows in Him that has flowed down through these generations." The evangelists give the genealogical tables and precisely according to them they also show at what different stages of evolution they stand. For Matthew, the important thing is to show that in Jesus of Nazareth we have a person in whom Father Abraham is living. The blood of Father Abraham has flowed down through the generations as far as Jesus. He thus traces the genealogical tables back to Abraham. He has a more materialistic point of view than Luke. The important thing for Luke was not alone to show that the God who lived in Abraham was present in Jesus, but that the ancestry, the line of descent, can be traced back still further, even to Adam and that Adam was a son of the very Godhead, which means that he belonged to the time when humanity had just made the transition from a spiritual to a physical state. Both Matthew and Luke wished to show that this earthly Jesus of Nazareth has His being only in what can be traced back to the divine Father-power. This was not a matter of importance for the writer of the Gospel of St. John who could gaze into the spiritual world. The important thing for him was not the words, "I and Father Abraham are one," but that at every moment of time, there exists in the human being an Eternal which was present in him before Father Abraham. This he wished to show. In the beginning was the Word which is called the "I AM." Before all external things and beings, He was. He was in the beginning. For those who wished rather to describe Jesus of Nazareth and were only able to describe him, it was a question of showing how from the beginning the blood flowed down through the generations. It was important to them to show that the same blood flowing down through the generations flowed also in Joseph, the father of Jesus.

If we could speak quite esoterically it would naturally be necessary to speak of the idea of the so-called "virgin birth," but this can be discussed only in the most intimate circles. It belongs to the deepest mysteries that exist and the misunderstanding connected with this idea arises because people do not know what is meant by the "virgin birth". They think that it means there was no fatherhood. But it is not that; a much more profound, a more mysterious something lies at the back of it which is quite compatible with what the other disciples wish to show, that is, that Joseph is the father of Jesus. If they were to deny this, then all the trouble they take to show this to be a fact would be meaningless. They wish to show that the ancient God exists in Jesus of Nazareth. Luke especially wished to make this very clear, therefore he traces the whole ancestry back to Adam and then to God. How could he have come to this conclusion, if he really wished only to say: I am showing you that this genealogical tree exists, but Joseph, as a matter of fact, had nothing to do with it. It would be very strange if people were to take the trouble to represent Joseph as a very important personality and then were to shove him aside out of the whole affair.

In the event of Palestine, we have not only to do with this highly developed personality, Jesus of Nazareth, who had passed through many incarnations, and had developed himself so highly that he needed such an extraordinary mother as the Virgin Sophia, but we have also to do with a second mystery. When Jesus of Nazareth was thirty years of age, he had advanced to such a stage through what he had experienced in his present incarnation that he could perform an action which it is possible for one to perform in exceptional cases. We know that the human being consists of physical, ether and astral bodies and an ego. This fourfold human being is the human being as he lives here among us. If a person stands at a certain high stage of evolution, it is possible for him at a particular moment to draw out his ego from the three bodies and abandon them, leaving them intact and entirely uninjured. This ego then goes into the spiritual worlds and the three bodies remain behind. We meet this process at times in cosmic evolution. At some especially exalted, enraptured moment, the ego of a person departs and enters into the spirit world—under certain conditions this can be extended over a long period—and because the three bodies are so highly developed by the ego that lived in them, they are fit instruments for a still higher being who now takes possession of them. In the thirtieth year of Jesus of Nazareth, that Being whom we have called the Christ, took possession of his physical, ether and astral bodies. This Christ Being could not incarnate in an ordinary child's body, but only in one which had first been prepared by a highly developed ego, for this Christ-Being had never before been incarnated in a physical body. Therefore from the thirtieth year on, we are dealing with the Christ in Jesus of Nazareth.

What in reality took place? The fact is that the corporality of Jesus of Nazareth which he had left behind was so mature, so perfect, that the Sun Logos, the Being of the six Elohim, which we have described as the spiritual Being of the Sun, was able to penetrate into it. It could incarnate for three years in this corporality, could become flesh. The Sun Logos Who can shine into human beings through illumination, the Sun Logos Himself, the Holy Spirit, entered. The Universal-Ego, the Cosmic Ego entered and from then on during three years, the Sun Logos spoke through the body of Jesus. The Christ speaks through the body of Jesus during these three years. This event is indicated in the Gospel of St. John and also in the other Gospels as the descent of the dove, of the Holy Spirit, upon Jesus of Nazareth. In esoteric Christianity it is said, that at that moment the ego of Jesus of Nazareth left his body, and that from then on the Christ is in him, speaking through him in order to teach and work. This is the first event that happens, according to the Gospel of St. John. We now have the Christ within the astral, ether and physical bodies of Jesus of Nazareth. There He worked as has been described until the Mystery of Golgotha occurred. What occurred on Golgotha? Let us consider that important moment when the blood flowed from the wounds of the Crucified Saviour. In order that you may understand me better, I shall compare what occurred with something else.

Let us suppose we have here a vessel filled with water. In the water, salt is dissolved and the water becomes quite transparent. Because we have warmed the water, we have made a salt solution. Now let us cool the water. The salt precipitates and we see how the salt condenses below and forms a deposit at the bottom of the vessel. That is the process for one who sees only with physical eyes. But for a person who can see with spiritual eyes, something else is happening. While the salt is condensing below, the spirit of the salt streams up through the water, filling it. The salt can only become condensed when the spirit of the salt has departed from it and become diffused into the water. Those who understand these things know that wherever condensation takes place, a spiritualization also always occurs. What thus condenses below has its counterpart above in the spiritual, just as in the case of the salt, when it condenses and is precipitated below, its spirit streams upward and disseminates. Therefore, it was not only a physical process that took place when the blood flowed from the wounds of the Saviour, but it was actually accompanied by a spiritual process; that is, the Holy Spirit which was received at the Baptism united Itself with the earth; that the Christ Himself flowed into the very being of the earth. From now on, the earth was changed, and this is the reason for saying to you, in earlier lectures, that if a person had viewed the earth from a distant star, he would have observed that its whole appearance was altered with the Mystery of Golgotha. The Sun Logos became a part of the earth, formed an alliance with it and became the Spirit of the Earth. This He achieved by entering into the body of Jesus of Nazareth in his thirtieth year, and by remaining active there for three years, after which He continued to remain on the earth. Now, the important thing is, that this Event must produce an effect upon the true Christian; that it must give something by which he may gradually develop the beginnings of a purified astral body in the Christian sense. There had to be something there for the Christian whereby he could make his astral body gradually more and more like a Virgin Sophia, and through it, receive into himself the Holy Spirit which was able to spread out over the entire earth, but which could not be received by anyone whose astral body did not resemble the Virgin Sophia. There had to be something which possesses the power to transform the human astral body into a Virgin Sophia. What is this power? It consists in the fact of Christ Jesus entrusting to the Disciple whom He loved—in other words to the writer of the Gospel of St. John—the mission of describing truly and faithfully through his own illumination the events of Palestine in order that men might be affected by them. If men permit what is written in the Gospel of St. John to work sufficiently upon them, their astral body is in the process of becoming a Virgin Sophia and it will become receptive to the Holy Spirit. Gradually, through the strength of the impulse which emanates from this Gospel, it will become susceptible of feeling the true spirit and later of perceiving it. This mission, this charge, was given to the writer of the Gospel by Jesus Christ. You need but read the Gospel. The Mother of Jesus—the Virgin Sophia in the esoteric meaning of Christianity—stands at the foot of the Cross, and from the Cross tne Christ says to the Disciple whom He loved: "Henceforth, this is thy Mother" and from this hour the Disciple took her unto himself. This means: "That force which was in My astral body and made it capable of becoming bearer of the Holy Spirit, I now give over to thee; thou shalt write down what this astral body has been able to acquire through its development." "And the Disciple took her unto himself," that means he wrote the Gospel of St. John. And this Gospel of St. John is the Gospel in which the writer has concealed powers which develop the Virgin Sophia. At the Cross, the mission was entrusted to him of receiving that force as his mother and of being the true, genuine interpreter of the Messiah. This really means that if you live wholly in accordance with the Gospel of St. John and understand it spiritually, it has the force to lead you to Christian katharsis, it has the power to give you the Virgin Sophia. Then will the Holy Spirit, united with the earth, grant you illumination or photismos according to the Christian meaning. And what the most intimate disciples experienced there in Palestine was so powerful that from that time on, they possessed at least the capacity of perceiving in the spiritual world. The most intimate disciples had received this capacity into themselves. Perceiving in the spirit, in the Christian sense, means that the person transforms his astral body to such a degree through the power of the Event of Palestine that what he sees need not be before him externally and physically-sensible. He possesses something by means of which he can perceive in the spirit. There were such intimate pupils. The woman who anointed the feet of Christ Jesus in Bethany had received through the Event of Palestine the powerful force needed for spiritual perception, and she is, for example, one of those who first understood that what had lived in Jesus was present after His death, that is, had been resurrected. She possessed this faculty. It may be asked: Whence came this possibility? It came through the development of her inner sense-organs. Are we told this in the Gospel? We are indeed; we are told that Mary Magdalene was led to the grave, that the body had disappeared and that she saw there two spiritual forms. These two spiritual forms are always to be seen when a corpse is present for a certain time after death. On the one side is to be seen the astral body, and on the other, what gradually separates from it as ether body, then passing over into the cosmic ether. Wholly apart from the physical body, there are two spiritual forms present which belong to the spiritual world.

Then the disciples went away again unto their own home. But Mary stood without at the sepulchre weeping; and as she wept she stooped down and looked into the sepulchre, and seeth two angels in white sitting.

She beheld this because she had become clairvoyant through the force and power of the Event of Palestine. And she beheld something more: she beheld the Risen Christ. Was it necessary for her to be clairvoyant, to be able to behold the Christ? If you have seen a person in physical form a few days ago, do you not think you would recognize him again if he should appear before you?

And when she had thus said, she turned herself back and saw Jesus standing and knew not that it was Jesus.

Jesus saith unto her, Woman why weepest thou? Whom seekest thou? She, supposing it to be the gardener . . . .

And in order that it might be told to us as exactly as possible, it was not only said once, but again at the next appearance of the Risen Christ, when Jesus appeared at the sea of Gennesareth.

But when the morning was now come, Jesus stood on the shore: but the disciples knew not that it was Jesus.

The esoteric pupils find Him there. Those who had received the full force of the Event of Palestine could grasp the situation and see that it was the

Risen Jesus who could be perceived spiritually. Although the disciples and Mary Magdalene saw Him, yet there were some among them who were less able to develop clairvoyant power. One of these was Thomas. It is said that he was not present the first time the disciples saw the Lord, and he declared he would have to lay his hands in His wounds, he would have to touch physically the body of the Risen Christ. You ask: What happened? The effort was then made to assist him to develop spiritual perception. And how was this done? Let us take the words of the Gospel itself:

> And after a week His disciples were again within, and Thomas with them: then came Jesus the doors being shut, and stood in their midst, and said, Peace be unto you.
>
> Then saith He to Thomas, reach hither thy fingers and behold My hands, and reach hither thy hand and thrust it into My side: and be not faithless, but believing. And thou shalt behold something if thou dost not rely upon the outer appearance, but art impregnated with inner power.

This inner power which should proceed from the Event of Palestine is called "Faith." It is no ordinary force, but an inner clairvoyant power. Permeate thyself with inner power, then thou needest no longer hold as real that only which thou seest externally; for blessed are they who are able to know what they do not see outwardly!

Thus we see that we have to do with the full reality and truth of the Resurrection and that only those are fully able to understand it, who have first developed the inner power to perceive in the spirit world. This will make the last chapter of the Gospel of St. John comprehensible to you, in which again and again it is pointed out that the closest followers of Christ Jesus have reached the stage of the Virgin Sophia, because the Event of Golgotha had been consummated in their presence. But when they had to stand firm for the first time, had actually to behold a spiritual event, they were still blinded and had first to find their way. They did not know that He was the same One Who had earlier been among them. Here is something which we must grasp with the most subtle concepts; for the grossly materialistic person would say: "Then the Resurrection is undermined!" The miracle of the Resurrection is to be taken quite literally, for

He said: "Lo, I remain with you always, even unto the end of the age, unto the end of the cosmic age."

He is there and will come again, although not in a form of flesh, but in a form in which those who have been sufficiently developed through the power of the Gospel of St. John, can actually perceive Him and possessing the power to perceive Him, they will no longer be unbelieving. The mission of the *Spiritual Science Movement* is to prepare those who have the will to allow themselves to be prepared, for the return of the Christ upon earth. This is the cosmo-historical significance of Spiritual Science, to prepare mankind and to keep its eyes open for the time when the Christ will appear again actively among men in the sixth cultural epoch, in order that that may be accomplished for a great part of humanity which was indicated to us in the Marriage at Cana.

Therefore the world-concept obtained from Spiritual Science appears like an execution of the testament of Christianity. In order to be lead to real Christianity, the men of the future will have to receive that spiritual teaching which Spiritual Science is able to give. Many people may still say today: Spiritual Science is something that really contradicts true Christianity. But those are the little popes who form opinions about things of which they know nothing and who make into a dogma: What I do not know does not exist.

This intolerance will become greater and greater in the future and Christianity will experience the greatest danger just from those people who, at present, believe they can be called good Christians. The Christianity of Spiritual Science will experience serious attacks from the Christians in name, for all concepts must change, if a true spiritual understanding of Christianity is to come about. Above all, the soul must become more and more conversant with and understanding of the legacy of the writer of the Gospel of St. John, the great school of the Virgin Sophia, the St. John's Gospel itself. Only Spiritual Science can lead us deeper into this Gospel.

In these lectures, only examples could be given showing how Spiritual Science can introduce us into the Gospel of St. John, for it is impossible to explain the whole of it. We read in the Gospel itself:

And there are also many other things which Jesus did; and I

suppose that were they all written down one after the other, the world could not contain all the books that would have to be written.

Just as the Gospel itself cannot go into all the details of the Event of Palestine, so too is it impossible for even the longest course of lectures to present the full spiritual content of the Gospel. Therefore we must be satisfied with those indications which could be given at this time; we must content ourselves with the thought that through just such indications in the course of human evolution, the true testament of Christianity becomes executed. Let us allow all this to have such an effect upon us that we may possess the power to hold fast to the foundation which we recognize in the Gospel of St. John, when others come to us and say: You are giving us too complicated concepts, too many concepts which we must first make our own in order to comprehend this Gospel: the Gospel is for the simple and naive and one dare not approach them with many concepts and thoughts. Many say this today. They perhaps refer to another saying: "Blessed are the poor in spirit, for theirs is the kingdom of heaven." One can merely quote such a saying as long as one does not understand it, for it really says: "Blessed are the beggars in spirit, for they shall reach the kingdom of heaven within themselves." This means that those who are like beggars of the spirit, who desire to receive more and more of the spirit, will find in themselves the kingdom of heaven!

At the present time the idea is all too prevalent that everything religious is identical with all that is primitive and simple. People say: We acknowledge that Science possesses many and complicated ideas, but we do not grant the same to Faith and Religion. Faith and Religion—so say many "Christians"—must be simple and naive! They demand this. And many rely upon a conception which is little quoted perhaps, but which in the present is haunting the minds of men and which Voltaire, one of the great teachers of materialism, has expressed in the words: "Whoever wishes to be a prophet must find believers, for what he asserts must be believed, and only what is simple, what is always repeated in its simplicity, that alone finds believers."

This is often so with the prophets, both true and false. They take the trouble to say something and to repeat it again and again and the people learn to believe it, because it is constantly repeated. The representative of Spiritual Science desires to be no such prophet. He does not wish to be a prophet at all. And although it may often be said: "Yes, you not only repeat, but you are always elucidating things from other sides, you are always discussing them in other ways;" when they speak thus to him, he is guilty of no fault. A prophet wishes that people believe in him. Spiritual Science has no desire to lead to *belief*, but to *knowledge*. Therefore let us take Voltaire's utterance in another way. He says:—"The *simple* is *believed* and is the concern of the prophet." Spiritual Science says:—the *manifold* is *known*. Let us try to understand more and more that Spiritual Science is something that is manifold—not a creed, but a path to knowledge, and consequently it bears within it the manifold. Therefore let us not shrink from collecting a great deal in order that we may understand one of the most important Christian documents, the Gospel of St. John. We have attempted to assemble the most varied material which places us in the position of being able to understand more and more the profound truths of this Gospel; able to understand how the physical mother of Jesus was an external manifestation, an external image of the Virgin Sophia; to understand what spiritual importance the Virgin Sophia had for the pupil of the Mysteries, whom the Christ loved; again to understand how, for the other Evangelists—who view the bodily descent of Jesus as important—the physical father plays his significant part when it was a question of the external imprint of the God-idea in the blood; and further, to understand what significance the Holy Spirit had for John, the Holy Spirit through which the Christ was begotten in the body of Jesus and dwelt therein during the three years and which is symbolized for us in the descent of the Dove at the Baptism by John.

If we understand that we must call the father of Christ Jesus the Holy Spirit who begot the Christ in the bodies of Jesus, then if we are able to comprehend a thing from all sides, we shall find it easy to understand that those disciples who were less highly initiated could not give us so profound a picture of the Events of Palestine as the Disciple whom the Lord loved. And if people, at present, speak of the Synoptics—which are the only authoritative Gospels for them—this only shows that they do not have the will to rise to an understanding of the true form of the Gospel of St. John. For everybody resembles the God he understands. If we try to make into a feeling, into an experience, what we can learn from Spiritual Science about the Gospel of St. John, we shall then find that this Gospel is not a text-book, *but a force which can be active within our souls.*

If these short lectures have aroused in you the feeling that this Gospel contains not only what we have been discussing here, but that indirectly, through the medium of words, it contains the force which can develop the soul itself further, then what was really intended in these lectures has been rightly understood. Because in them, not only was something intended for the understanding, for the intellectual capacity of understanding, but that which takes its round-about path through this intellectual capacity of understanding should condense into feelings and inner experiences, and these feelings and experiences should be a result of the facts that have been presented here. If, in a certain sense, this has been rightly understood, we shall also comprehend what is meant when it is said that the Movement for Spiritual Science has the mission of raising Christianity into Wisdom, of rightly understanding Christianity, indirectly through spiritual wisdom. We shall understand that Christianity is only in the beginning of its activity, and its true mission will be fulfilled when it is understood in its true spiritual form. The more these lectures are understood in this way, the more have they been comprehended in the sense in which they were intended.

DATE DUE

GAYLORD			PRINTED IN U.S.A.